RISING TO LEAD

Stories of Rising Beyond the Ordinary

VIJAYALAKSHMI BABUKUMAR

INDIA • SINGAPORE • MALAYSIA

ISBN
Paperback 979-8-89673-478-9
Hardcase 979-8-89699-343-8

TABLE OF CONTENTS

INTRODUCTION

What does it mean to be a leader?

This question makes us pause and think about what leadership really means at its core. It's a question I have wrestled with throughout my own leadership journey, one that has shaped my experiences and, ultimately, led to the creation of this book. These pages are an attempt to explore this question, to move closer to understanding the depth and complexity of what it means to lead.

Leadership is often defined in simple terms—the ability to lead, influence, or guide others. While this definition provides a starting point, it only scratches the surface. Leadership is far more nuanced, more dynamic, and deeply rooted in human connection. Over time, our understanding of leadership has evolved, reflecting the changing nature of society and the complexities of the roles leaders play.

The modern perspective recognizes that effective leadership can emerge from anyone, at any level, who has the ability to inspire, motivate, and guide others toward a shared purpose. This shift has opened the door to more inclusive and dynamic approaches to leadership, where qualities like empathy, adaptability, and ethical decision-making take center stage.

Amidst the evolving understanding of leadership, it becomes evident that traditional narratives often fall short of capturing its true complexity. Much of the older literature tends to glorify a one-dimensional view of success, emphasizing authority, achievements, and the ability to meet organizational goals. While these aspects are important, they offer an incomplete picture of what leadership entails. The human elements—struggles, failures, resilience—are often left out of the story, leaving aspiring leaders with an unrealistic portrayal of what it means to lead.

The problem with these traditional portrayals is not just that they are incomplete but that they can be discouraging. Aspiring leaders who encounter setbacks may feel inadequate if their experiences don't align with these idealized notions. It paints success as linear and straightforward rather than the dynamic, iterative process it truly is. Leaders face ambiguity, they make mistakes, and they grow from these experiences. Ignoring these realities risks perpetuating a myth of perfection that leaves no room for vulnerability or learning.

By focusing solely on outcomes, traditional narratives also fail to prepare leaders for the resilience needed in today's fast-paced world. The ability to bounce back from failures, adapt to new challenges, and learn from missteps is critical for effective leadership; without acknowledging the importance of this adaptability, leadership literature risks leaving individuals unprepared for the realities of leading in environments that demand constant evolution.

This book aims to bridge the gap between the idealized portrayals of leadership and the real, often messy experiences that come with leading in complex and unpredictable environments. Leadership is often romanticized as being all about confident decisions, flawless execution, and constant success. In reality, leadership is much more human. It is full of dilemmas, setbacks, and moments of doubt, elements that rarely get mentioned in traditional narratives but are crucial to understanding what it really takes to lead effectively.

For anyone looking to grow as a leader, seeing the real side of leadership is so important. It helps dismantle the myth that you have to be perfect to lead well. Instead, what makes a good leader are qualities like resilience, empathy, and the ability to adapt when things don't go as planned. The stories in this book reflect that. They show that great leadership doesn't come from always getting it right; it comes from learning through the struggles, reflecting on mistakes, and growing through each experience. That's where the real power lies—not in never failing, but in always finding a way to learn and move forward.

These stories also provide valuable lessons that often come through most clearly during times of struggle. They offer insight into how to handle uncertainty, recover after setbacks, and lead with honesty and authenticity, even when things are tough. For example, when a leader shares how they rebuilt trust after making a significant mistake, it is an actionable lesson in resilience, trust-building, and growth. These lessons matter because they are drawn from real experiences. They move beyond abstract concepts and show what leadership looks like in practice, with all its imperfections and opportunities for growth.

To help you engage fully with the lessons and insights in this book, it has been structured into two sections, each with a distinct purpose. The first section brings you into the heart of authentic leadership stories. These are real, unfiltered accounts of what it means to lead—stories that show the highs and lows, the triumphs and setbacks, and the creativity and resilience it takes to navigate challenges. These narratives are not about perfection; they are about growth, humanity, and the personal journeys that shape effective leaders. At the end of each chapter in this first section, you'll find practical exercises designed to bridge these lessons to your own context. These exercises encourage action, helping you try out new approaches, develop key skills, and embrace a mindset that is open to creativity and inclusion. By applying these exercises, you can start experimenting with how these lessons might shape the way you lead, making them tangible and actionable in your everyday work.

The second section moves beyond traditional leadership examples to explore lessons from everyday encounters and unexpected sources. This part of the book highlights how leadership wisdom can emerge in the most surprising moments—from interactions with colleagues, guidance from mentors, or even quiet observations in daily life. Each chapter here ends with reflection questions. These are not simple prompts—they are invitations to think deeply about how these stories connect to your own experiences. The goal is to encourage you to draw lessons that feel personal and relevant, helping you consider how these insights might apply to the situations you face in your leadership journey.

To get the most out of this book, approach each section with curiosity and an open mind. Let the exercises in the first section push you to apply the stories in practical ways, and use the reflection questions in the second section to deepen your understanding and insight. This is not a rigid manual or a one-size-fits-all guide. It is a resource to help you uncover and refine your own path as a leader. Each time you face a new challenge or milestone, the insights in these pages may offer something fresh, resonating differently as your perspective grows. Use it as a tool to refine how you lead, ensuring that your leadership approach remains authentic to who you are while adapting to the ever-changing world around you.

And as we step into this journey together, let's recall the words of T.S. Eliot: "Every moment is a fresh beginning."

Embrace this beginning with enthusiasm and curiosity, for it is the start of a deeper, more profound understanding of what it truly means to lead.

Section 1

VOICES OF LEADERSHIP: STORIES FROM THE FRONT LINES

Chapter 1

UNCONVENTIONAL PATHS

Ralph Nader once said, "I start with the premise that the function of leadership is to produce more leaders, not more followers." These words hit home for me as I think back on one of the most inspiring leaders I've ever had the honour of knowing. We were classmates in school, but as life often does, it took us in different directions. In the years that followed, she set out on a journey marked by learning, growth, and leadership, eventually becoming a shining example of inspiration.

She began her journey as a homemaker, devoted to raising her two children and ensuring their education was her top priority. Every day, a tutor would come to their home, and she would sit in on the lessons, keenly observing and participating to make sure her children were getting the most out of their studies. Even then, she had a dream—a quiet desire to start something of her own. But, like many dreams, it was clouded with uncertainty. She didn't know where to begin or what exactly she wanted to pursue.

Then, one day, a casual conversation with the tutor became the spark that would ignite her leadership journey. The tutor mentioned that the school she worked at was being put up for sale. The owners were elderly, and without a successor to take over, they were ready to let go of the institution. It was as if the universe had handed her the opportunity she had been searching for, albeit wrapped in uncertainty and challenge.

When her tutor gently suggested she consider taking over a local school, she laughed it off. "Running a school is the last thing I'd ever do," she said with a sigh. Her journey had been unconventional—marrying young and stepping away from college just shy of graduating, she felt disconnected from the academic world. The notion of leading a school seemed out of reach, more aligned with someone who held formal degrees and traditional credentials.

But her tutor wouldn't back down, pointing out how effortlessly she engaged with her children's learning. "You might not have a degree, but you teach and care for your children as if you've mastered education," her tutor insisted. This perspective shift sparked a flicker of possibility in her mind.

The real test came on December 5, 2008, a day that marked her transition from doubt to leadership. Standing in front of 350 parents at the newly acquired school, her voice trembled as she introduced herself not just as the new owner but as a dedicated guardian of their children's education. "I will take care of your children and their learning," she promised, a pledge she has honoured ever since.

Years have passed since that day, and the seeds of courage she planted have grown into something remarkable. Today, she is the founder of not just one but three schools—Vivekananda Matriculation School, Vivekananda Public School, and IRA Montessori Hub. The woman who once questioned her capability to lead has now become a pillar of education in her community, showing everyone that leadership isn't about the diplomas on your wall but about having the guts to step forward and the resolve to create change.

Her name is Padmini Ramamoorthy, and her journey from a hesitant homemaker to a respected educator underscores the power of believing in oneself, even when the odds seem overwhelming.

When I spoke with her, she shared a pivotal moment in her journey. "After we acquired the primary school, we decided to expand by offering secondary education starting from 6th grade. This decision came with encouragement from the same teacher who had initially pushed me to buy the school. We had discussions with the education board, and based on those talks, we went ahead and started the 6th grade, even though we were still waiting for the official approval."

Things seemed to be moving forward until a student requested a transfer certificate because her family needed to relocate. It was at this moment that they realized they were in serious trouble. The approval they were counting on from the education board was delayed, and to make matters worse, the commissioner who had promised to facilitate the approval was suddenly transferred. They were left in a state of uncertainty, with no clear path forward.

It was in that moment of crisis that she made a crucial decision. "I realized that if something needs to be done, I have to dive into the details myself and make personal connections with the necessary officials." This decision marked a turning point in her leadership journey, teaching her the importance of taking charge, understanding every aspect of the work, and building the relationships needed to see things through. It was a lesson in resilience and persistence, qualities that have since become hallmarks of her leadership style.

Continuing her reflections on navigating through challenges, she delved into how the pandemic tested their adaptability. "Like many schools, we initially struggled to shift to online classes. It was a daunting task to get all the children and teachers accustomed to this new way of learning," she recounted. However, the community's spirit shone brightly during these times. "The support from parents was truly remarkable. In neighborhoods where some families lacked the necessary technology, others opened their homes, allowing groups of children to attend online classes together. It was heartening to see how quickly everyone adapted, ensuring that no child was left behind."

She also shared a personal anecdote that highlighted the value of foresight and preparation, virtues instilled in her from a young age. "Growing up in a joint family, my grandmother always emphasized the importance of saving for the future. This lesson proved invaluable during the pandemic," she said. Thanks to her prudent financial management, she was able to ensure that all her staff and teachers were taken care of during those uncertain times. "Having sufficient funds set aside allowed us to support our entire team without interruption, despite the challenges," she added.

This mix of community support and personal preparedness helped her school tackle the initial shock of the pandemic, reinforcing the strength of collective effort and the impact of long-term planning in overcoming adversity.

Building on her reflections about overcoming challenges during the pandemic, she also places great importance on having a clear mission, vision, and values within her organization. However, for her, the real significance lies in how these principles are actively followed and translated into meaningful actions that benefit society. At her school, the focus is on creating equal opportunities for all children. Recognizing that some students face significant hardships, she has introduced counseling sessions to help them handle their difficulties and regain their confidence and energy. Special care is given to students who require more attention, ensuring that everyone has the support they need to thrive.

Exploring her leadership style reveals that her approach focuses on achieving goals while also enabling the development of every individual in the organization. She advocates for a philosophy centred on identifying unique skills and matching them with appropriate roles. This approach promotes a positive work environment and ensures everyone has the chance to excel. This philosophy has cultivated a loyal and committed team, evidencing the power of her simple yet profound principle: a peaceful and supportive atmosphere leads to mutual respect and collective success.

This commitment to building a strong, supportive team aligns with her deeper understanding of leadership and life. As she puts it, "I see myself as the sculptor of my own life, guided by a strong belief in my intuition. One of the most profound lessons I've learned is that when you genuinely love and see people for who they truly are, this habit deepens, allowing you to connect with their souls on a meaningful level." For her, true leadership begins with this soulful connection, and she believes that investing time in building and nurturing a team creates bonds that last a lifetime. This soulful connection and deep-seated trust are what empowers her team to achieve beyond expectations, confirming her belief that when people feel genuinely seen and trusted, they deliver their best.

Her dedication to her principles shines through in how she faces life's unavoidable hurdles. Given these pressures, it's remarkable how she keeps her balance and remains steadfast. For her, the key lies in strategic planning and disciplined routines. She shared some of the strategies that have guided her through tough times: "Balancing the demands of children, health, work, and home has always been my priority. To make it all work, I've embraced the early mornings, finding time for exercise and completing tasks before my children even wake up." Her routine is a testament to her commitment, not just to her professional role but to her personal life as well. By investing time wisely and making sacrifices, she maintains that these are the necessary ingredients for success in all areas of life, demonstrating that true leadership involves constant balance and adaptation.

She is a firm believer in the power of mind mapping, both in her personal and professional life. Before diving into any task, she lays out all possible options, carefully weighing the pros and cons. This practice helps her anticipate challenges and tackle them more effectively. Physical well-being also plays a crucial role in her routine. Every day, she makes it a point to walk 10,000 steps, believing that exercise is a direct route to happiness. She has found that maintaining a healthy body, mind, and soul is essential to being truly content.

For her, choosing happiness is intentional, shaped by mindfulness and a strong personal ethic. She shares, "I'm always clear and consistent in my views. My perspective doesn't change with circumstances or the people I'm with. What you see is exactly who I am." This consistency brings purpose and joy to everything she does, energizing her efforts and making her daily actions meaningful. She enriches her own life and becomes a powerful source of inspiration and effective leadership for everyone around her by tackling every task with intention and heart.

Conceptualizing the Essence of Padmini Ramamoorthy's Leadership

As we delve deeper into the leadership journey of Padmini Ramamoorthy, it becomes clear that her approach is a unique blend of *servant leadership* and *transformational leadership*, wrapped in resilience and personal balance.

Leading Through Service

Padmini's leadership is rooted in the belief that true leaders are those who serve first. Her focus on the growth and well-being of her students and staff stands out as a defining trait. She dedicates herself to creating equal opportunities, ensuring access to counseling, and fostering a community where everyone feels supported.

Inspiring Growth and Change

But Padmini's leadership goes beyond service—it's also about transformation. Her journey from being a homemaker to founding and leading a school underscores her ability to inspire and motivate others to reach beyond their perceived limits. She doesn't just maintain the status quo; she pushes for innovation and change, encouraging those around her to grow and evolve. This transformational aspect of her leadership is what drives her school to continuously adapt and improve.

Overcoming Challenges

Throughout her journey, Padmini has shown remarkable resilience and adaptability, consistently overcoming challenges like bureaucratic hurdles for school approvals and the sudden need for online teaching during the pandemic. Her ability to adapt swiftly and effectively to these changing circumstances underscores her exceptional leadership qualities.

Empathy and Compassion

Building on this adaptability, Padmini prioritizes understanding and nurturing her team. By empathizing and stepping into someone else's shoes, she gains a broader perspective that enriches her leadership approach. When addressing staff errors, instead of issuing reprimands, she opts for a more constructive approach. Recognizing that childhood traumas can influence behaviour, she carefully explains alternative actions, inspiring learning and strengthening bonds within her team. This compassionate approach has secured a lasting loyalty from her staff, enhancing the collective resilience of her organization.

A Holistic Approach

Padmini's leadership philosophy extends beyond immediate problem-solving to encompass self-care, self-respect, and self-love as fundamental tenets of her daily routine. By prioritizing these principles, she ensures her own well-being and sets a powerful example for her team. This holistic approach to leadership cements her role as a transformative leader and demonstrates how balanced living can significantly contribute to sustained professional success and a harmonious work environment.

From Vision to Action: Emulating the Leadership Excellence of Padmini Ramamoorthy

To effectively follow in the footsteps of Padmini Ramamoorthy's leadership, aspiring leaders can adopt key strategies that inspire growth and meaningful change.

Prioritizing Service for Team Growth

The journey begins with prioritizing service—focusing on the needs and development of your team. This involves actively listening, providing support, and empowering each member to reach their full potential. Equally important is the value of respect in leadership. Understanding and appreciating the differences within your team can simplify managing and resolving challenges. If respect is lacking for any reason, it may be better to part ways with those individuals, as respect is fundamental to maintaining a healthy and effective team dynamic. Ensuring that the well-being of your team is at the core of every decision is essential for cultivating a positive and productive work environment.

Inspiring Change

Moreover, aspiring leaders should strive to inspire and transform. By articulating a compelling vision, you can inspire others to embrace change and innovation. This involves inspiring an environment ripe for creativity, where each individual feels driven to contribute their best, thereby transforming the collective output and workplace culture.

Building Resilience

Resilience is another cornerstone of effective leadership. Developing the ability to adapt swiftly to changes and navigate through challenges is crucial. It's about seeing obstacles as opportunities to learn and grow. This mindset is instrumental in building a resilient leadership style that can withstand the pressures and unpredictability of the modern world.

A balanced approach to life and leadership is equally important. Maintaining a healthy equilibrium between personal well-being and professional duties ensures sustainability and fulfillment. This balance allows for setting clear priorities, managing time efficiently, and dedicating adequate resources to nourish both personal and professional aspects of life.

Nurturing a Supportive Culture

Lastly, creating a supportive culture within the organization is vital. This involves nurturing a workplace where trust, collaboration, and mutual respect are paramount. Encouraging open communication, providing resources for continuous development, and building a community that supports each other's growth are all practices that forge a strong, united team.

Exercise: Reflective Leadership Mapping

As you reflect on the inspiring journey of Padmini Ramamoorthy, it's time to take a step forward and apply the lessons from her leadership style to your own path. The following exercise is designed to help you internalize the principles of servant and transformational leadership that Padmini exemplifies. By working through this framework, you'll align your personal leadership values with actionable steps that resonate deeply with your role as a leader.

To help you integrate the principles of servant and transformational leadership into your daily practices, we will map out your personal leadership values and actions.

Step 1: Vision Articulation

- Start by giving yourself 15 minutes of uninterrupted time. Use this moment to quietly reflect on your vision as a leader. What is the change you want to create in your organization or community? Allow this vision to take shape in your mind, and then capture it in a clear, concise statement that truly reflects your aspirations.

Step 2: Servant Leadership Assessment

- Consider three ways you currently serve your team or community. For each one, identify a specific area where you could deepen your support or empower others more effectively.

- Think about a recent decision you made as a leader. Revisit this decision through the lens of servant leadership: Did it prioritize the growth and well-being of others? Reflect on how you might approach similar decisions in the future to better serve those you lead.

____

____

____

____

____

____

____

____

____

____

Step 3: Transformational Leadership Challenge

- Identify a challenge or opportunity for innovation within your sphere of influence. Design a small, actionable initiative that encourages creative thinking and involves your team in the process.

- Set a timeline for this initiative and define what success will look like. Consider how you will inspire and motivate your team to embrace this challenge and work together towards a shared goal.

Step 4: Resilience and Adaptability Journaling

- Reflect on a past experience where you demonstrated resilience. Write a brief journal entry about what you learned from that situation and how it shaped your approach to leadership.

- Look ahead to a current or upcoming challenge. Develop a flexible plan that incorporates resilience, identifying potential obstacles and how you'll navigate them.

Step 5: Balance and Well-being Plan

- Create a balance sheet that lists your key personal and professional commitments. For each area, identify one action you can take to ensure they are aligned and mutually supportive.

- Establish a weekly routine that includes time for self-care and reflection. This is about ensuring that your leadership responsibilities are balanced with your personal life, keeping you grounded and fulfilled.

____

____

____

____

____

____

____

____

____

____

Step 6: Follow-Up

- Once you've completed this exercise, schedule a conversation with a trusted mentor or colleague to discuss your insights and action plans. Use their feedback to refine your strategies and gather additional perspectives. This discussion will strengthen your commitment and provide you with valuable support as you continue to grow as a leader.

____

____

____

____

____

____

____

____

____

____

____

Wrapping up the reflective leadership mapping exercise, you may have tapped into deeper insights about your own leadership style and values. This journey of self-discovery is far from over; it marks the beginning of a continuous evolution in leadership—learning, adapting, and growing with each experience.

An essential insight to carry forward is making peace your guiding principle in every task. This shift in perspective can transform your approach to life, helping you avoid unnecessary conflicts and inspiring a more harmonious existence both personally and professionally. Leadership is an ever-evolving process, and embracing peace as a core goal can profoundly influence how you lead and live.

Chapter 2

COOL, CALM, AND CRUSHING IT

There are phrases about leadership that resonate long after they're spoken. One such phrase from Robin Sharma stands out to me: "Leadership is not about a title or a designation. It's about impact, influence, and inspiration." These words often echo in my thoughts, especially when I reflect on the incredible impact of a leader who shaped my professional trajectory and left a profound imprint on how I view the essence of leadership.

This leader, working in the fast-paced marketing industry, was unlike any marketing professional I have ever met. While many in marketing can often be seen as all talk, fixated on numbers and stressed about closing deals, he was different.

He had a knack for cutting through the noise of typical industry pressures and focusing on what truly mattered—authentic connections and sustainable results. It was all about sparking meaningful connections that built lasting value for the brand and real happiness for our clients. His approach to leadership and marketing was about building relationships and setting a calm, yet determined, tone for his team. His presence brought a sense of stability and confidence that permeated throughout our department, influencing our actions and inspiring our aspirations.

This empowered many of us to exceed our personal and professional goals, frequently leading to accomplishments beyond our imagination.

By now, you're probably curious to find out who I'm referring to. His name is Mr Pankaj Kapoor, Vice President at Cummins India. He is a mechanical engineer from Arya Bhatt Institute of Technology and holds an MBA in Sales and Marketing from AIMA. When he joined the company, he already had over 25 years of industry experience, bringing a wealth of knowledge and expertise.

Let me take you back to my early encounters with him at the company where we both worked. It was 2005, and during his tenure, the company underwent a significant transformation. Under his leadership, we experienced an impressive 5X growth year after year, with a positive and robust P&L that delighted our customers. Over the course of a decade, he was the driving force behind taking the business from a 50 Cr turnover to an astounding 2,500 Cr.

His leadership style was inclusive and empowering. He actively encouraged every team member to share their ideas and contribute to the company's sustainability and growth. This approach made each individual feel like an essential part of the whole.

Customer service was another area where his strategic approach excelled. He insisted that any customer issue be discussed thoroughly among the team. These collaborative problem-solving sessions involved brainstorming and collective decision-making, leading to innovative solutions and nurturing a sense of unity and shared purpose. Every challenge was a learning opportunity, and every solution a team victory.

One of my most personal and profound experiences under his leadership highlighted his forward-thinking and inclusive approach. Despite the presence of numerous male candidates for a particular management role, he championed diversity by advocating for my candidacy—a decision typically unsupported in our male-dominated industry. He saw my potential and aimed to shatter traditional biases, giving me the opportunity to demonstrate my skills and contribute meaningfully to the team. His actions strongly underscored his dedication to nurturing talent, irrespective of gender.

Conceptualizing the Essence of Pankaj Kapoor's Leadership

As we delve deeper into his approach to leadership, it becomes clear that his style is deeply rooted in *mindful leadership* and *customer-focused leadership*. These methods are more than buzzwords; they are crucial to how he guides his team and drives the business toward success.

Mindful Leadership

At the core of Mindful Leadership is the practice of being fully present and aware—qualities he embodies in every interaction. His calm and composed demeanor is about being genuinely centered. He listens attentively and responds with empathy and compassion, understanding the nuanced needs of his team members. This open and transparent communication ensures that no ideas are lost in translation, and everyone feels heard and respected.

His authenticity extends to how he leads. He is not afraid to adapt and innovate, constantly looking for ways to improve processes and outcomes. His leadership is dynamic, capable of pivoting and reinventing solutions to meet the ever-changing demands of the business world.

Customer-Focused Leadership

Turning to his customer-focused leadership, it's evident that he places immense value on understanding and prioritizing customer needs. This customer-centric approach goes beyond focusing on cultivating relationships that nurture trust and loyalty. He empowers his team to make decisions that enhance customer satisfaction, ensuring that they have the authority and confidence to act decisively.

The trust he cultivates, combined with a steadfast focus on customer satisfaction, drives the company to remarkable achievements and sets a high standard for leadership.

Through his leadership example, we see how effective leadership is about guiding with a gentle hand and a clear vision, nurturing relationships, and always placing collective well-being at the forefront of every action. It is a powerful reminder of what we can aspire to achieve in our roles, no matter the industry or scope of work.

This ethos of perseverance and collective well-being naturally leads us deeper into his personal philosophy. His guiding principle is straightforward yet profound: "Perseverance is the quality to carry forward in life."

Life's path is strewn with challenges, particularly when you aim high. He believes that it's not the obstacles themselves, but how you respond to them that defines your journey. There will be times when others may doubt you, attempt to hinder your progress, or even actively work against you. In such times, the clarity of your commitment becomes crucial.

He also advocates for a dynamic approach to leadership: *Always winning is not important, but always reinventing yourself to meet current needs and finding innovative solutions is key to success.* He emphasizes that *the value you bring to the table goes beyond outcomes; it's also about how you adapt and evolve.* When you continuously seek ways to improve and respond to changing circumstances with innovative thinking, you set yourself and your team up for long-term success.

Furthermore, he highlights the importance of valuing people and customers alike. This dual focus ensures that while you're innovating and adapting, you're also staying grounded in the human aspect of business. Understanding and prioritizing the needs and well-being of both your team and your customers can lead to more meaningful and sustainable business practices.

From Vision to Action: Emulating the Leadership Excellence of Pankaj Kapoor

As you reflect on these principles and consider how to incorporate them into your own leadership style, let's focus on actionable steps you can take to embody these aspects in your daily leadership practices.

For Mindful Leadership

Practice Presence and Awareness

Engage fully wherever you are, whether it's a team meeting or a one-on-one. Really listen to what's being said and what might not be said, making each interaction more meaningful and productive.

Develop Empathy and Compassion

Strive to connect with your team on a personal level. Understand their challenges and aspirations, and support them in their professional growth and personal well-being.

Value People

Recognize and celebrate the individual strengths each team member brings to the table. This recognition boosts morale and motivates your team to contribute their best.

Maintain Authenticity and Transparency

Keep your communications honest and open. Sharing your own challenges and how you're addressing them can demystify leadership and inspire your team to tackle their own challenges with confidence.

Embrace Adaptability and Innovation

Encourage your team to bring forward new ideas and be open to experimenting with them. Sometimes, the most innovative solutions come from unexpected sources.

For Customer-Focused Leadership

Adopt a Customer-Centric Mindset

Make decisions with the customer in mind. Encourage your team to consider how their work impacts the customer experience and what changes might enhance it.

Understand Customer Needs

Spend time getting to know your customers beyond just the surface. This deeper understanding will guide better product development, more targeted marketing, and improved service delivery.

Empower Your Team

Trust your team to have autonomy when making decisions. This empowerment speeds up processes, instilling a sense of ownership and responsibility among team members.

Build Strong Customer Relationships

Cultivate lasting relationships through consistent and dependable customer interactions. Ensuring that your team understands the value of trust and reliability can set your business apart from competitors.

Delegate Authority

Encourage team members to take charge of projects. This develops their skills and shows trust in their abilities, creating a more dynamic and capable team.

Start by implementing one or two of these practices and gradually build from there. Over time, you'll likely see a more motivated team, improved results and stronger customer relationships. This kind of leadership transformation begins with you and can profoundly influence both the culture and success of your organization.

Exercise: Leadership Self-Assessment and Action Plan

Now's the time to take a closer look at your own leadership journey and see how the lessons we've discussed can shape it. This Leadership Self-Assessment and Action Plan is designed to help you evaluate your current leadership qualities and set a clear path for personal and professional growth. Embrace this opportunity to reflect, plan, and engage with your team in a meaningful way.

Step 1: Self-Assessment

Reflect on the following questions and write down your thoughts:

- **Presence and Awareness**
  - How often do you practice being fully present in your interactions with your team?
  - What steps can you take to improve your mindfulness in the workplace?

- **Empathy and Compassion**
  - How well do you understand the personal and professional needs of your team members?
  - What actions can you take to show more empathy and support?

- **Authenticity and Transparency**
  - How transparent are you in your communications with your team?
  - What can you do to build more trust through honesty and openness?

- **Customer-Centric Approach**
  - How well do you understand your customers' needs and challenges?
  - What strategies can you implement to enhance customer satisfaction?

- **Empowerment and Innovation**
  - How often do you encourage your team to share their ideas and take ownership of their roles?
  - What can you do to foster a more innovative and empowered team environment?

Step 2: Action Plan

Based on your self-assessment, create an action plan with specific steps to improve your leadership qualities:

- **Set Clear Goals**
  - Identify one or two areas where you want to improve (e.g., being more present and showing more empathy).
  - Set specific, measurable goals for these areas.
- **Develop Strategies**
  - Outline the strategies you will use to achieve your goals (e.g., practicing active listening, holding regular one-on-one meetings with team members).
- **Implement and Reflect**
  - Implement your strategies over the next month.
  - Reflect on your progress at the end of the month and adjust your action plan as needed.

____

____

____

____

____

____

Step 3: Team Feedback

Engage your team in the process:

- **Gather Feedback**
  - Ask your team for feedback on your leadership style and areas for improvement.
  - Use this feedback to refine your action plan.
- **Encourage Participation**
  - Encourage your team members to conduct their own self-assessments and create action plans.
  - Foster a culture of continuous improvement and mutual support.

This exercise is about strengthening your bond with your team and getting in tune with what your customers really need. Reflect on your own journey and the changes you can make to become the leader you aspire to be.

Take these insights to heart and think about how you can implement them in your daily interactions. After all, isn't the true measure of leadership not just in the success we achieve, but in the legacy we leave behind?

____

____

____

____

____

____

Chapter 3

STRATEGY, SACRIFICE, AND SUCCESS

Football Coach Vince Lombardi once said, "Leaders are not born; rather, they are created through hard work, just like any other skill. These words ring true as I think back to a formidable figure whose story embodies this very idea. Every great leader's tale starts with an unyielding drive and perseverance, and his story is no exception. Let me take you back to where it all started. His journey kicked off during the nascent stages of my own career and had a profound impact on me.

I began my career in the late '90s when I landed my first job as an operating engineer at an automotive company. Fresh out of college with a diploma in Mechanical Engineering, I was eager to make my mark in the industry. It was through a senior from college that I was introduced to him, who was then working at an automotive giant in the region. At that time, the leader was a tool room engineer at one of India's leading commercial vehicle manufacturers.

He was a whirlwind of activity, always on the move, juggling his responsibilities with remarkable efficiency. Meeting him was a rare occurrence due to his busy schedule and our paths rarely crossed during the hectic weekdays. It wasn't until one leisurely weekend that I had the chance to talk with him. That conversation illuminated so much about him, piecing together the image of a professional whose dedication was as commendable as it was rigorous.

He was working towards a Mechanical Engineering degree at a local college, skillfully balancing his academic and professional responsibilities by attending daytime classes and working evening shifts at his job. His routine was a rigorous one: classes started at 8:30 AM, and right after his college ended at 4 PM, he would dash home. Home was a brief pit stop where he switched from his college attire to his work uniform, making it to his second shift on time. He diligently followed this intense routine for three years.

I often marveled at his commitment. How could someone adhere so strictly to such a demanding schedule? One day, driven by curiosity and admiration, I asked him directly. The conversation that followed was enlightening. He shared his views on the indispensable value of education and the importance of continually updating our skills and knowledge to advance in our careers.

He told me, "To stay in the race of career and life, you must keep moving. If you rest, you risk falling behind. There's always someone else striving to outpace you and move ahead." His advice was simple yet profound: "Just keep taking small steps forward every day, and gradually, you'll reach your milestones."

These words were a lifeline thrown to me at a time when I was questioning my own path. Seeing him so animated, so certain, sparked something in me—a desire to emulate his tenacity and to harness the same fervor in my pursuits. It was this specific inspiration that drove me to actively push my boundaries. I went on to complete my BTech and MBA, each step forward fueled by the memory of his dedication and the realization that progress, no matter how incremental, builds over time.

Years slipped by like pages in a book, and it was almost two decades later when our paths crossed again—this time digitally, on LinkedIn. There, proudly displayed in bold letters, was a name I would never forget: Mr. Kennady Varghese. Next to his name was a title that filled me with awe yet didn't come as a surprise: Country Manager of a leading firm in the wind turbine sector. Knowing his relentless drive and dedication, it felt almost inevitable that he would ascend to such heights.

Over the years, he skillfully shaped his career path with purpose and foresight. He armed himself with crucial learning through an Executive General Management Program and an Advanced Management Program in Business, Marketing, and Related Support Services. These educational milestones were deliberate steps that prepared him to handle the complex demands of the global business world.

In his role as Country Manager, his impact was profound. Under his leadership, the company grew and set new benchmarks for excellence. This accolade upheld the company's high standards and his skillful leadership.

Reflecting on his journey from a dedicated engineering student to a leading figure in the industry really hits close to home for me. Every day, he committed himself to learning more, doing better, and pushing the boundaries of what he could achieve. Seeing his transformation up close, I've been touched by how his steadfast dedication and clear vision carved a path to his impressive achievements.

Recently, I reconnected with him, who has evolved into a seasoned leader. Our conversation naturally veered into the key experiences that have shaped his extraordinary career journey. I was curious to know if there was a defining moment he could pinpoint, but his response illuminated the broader truth of his journey. "There's not just one defining moment," he said thoughtfully. "It's more about the consistency in your efforts, the small yet significant improvements you make every day—both in your professional life and as an individual—that help you overcome challenges."

He elaborated on the essence of leadership as the capacity to manage complex situations effectively, especially when working across various sectors and product lines. "Leadership demands that you grasp the big picture while also diving into the operational details," he explained, his voice steady and assured. "In a fast-paced and dynamic economy like India's, you have to be adept at tackling both ends of this spectrum."

His deep knowledge of every functional area within his industry enables him to nurture a genuine connection with his team, guiding them towards collective excellence with empathy and understanding.

This conversation with him was like stepping into a masterclass on leadership as it unfolded. As we talked, it became clear that his approach has always been about more than just overseeing operations; it's about nurturing and valuing the people within them. He emphasized how recognizing the hard work and humility of his team, and always ensuring credit is given where it's due, forms the cornerstone of a thriving workplace. "It's about creating an environment where inquiry is encouraged, and every decision is backed by data and thoughtful analysis," he explained. This careful approach inspires trust and cements respect among team members, paving the way for a cohesive and forward-moving organizational culture.

He passionately spoke about the necessity of continuous growth—both personal and professional. As someone who never stops learning, he highlighted how keeping abreast with new knowledge and insights has been essential in maintaining his effectiveness as a leader. "We're constantly enriching ourselves by engaging with everyone around us—our colleagues, our customers," he shared. "It's about being deeply immersed in our roles, approaching each day with passion and an open mind."

This conversation served as a profound reminder of what true leadership looks like. For those of us looking to lead, his path offers a valuable blueprint: leadership is about investing wholeheartedly in your own development and nurturing the potential of those around you.

Conceptualizing the Essence of Kennady Varghese's Leadership

As we delve deeper into his philosophies and nature of leadership, it becomes clear that his approach is ***transformative***. His ability to inspire, motivate, and nurture an environment of continuous improvement and innovation has been the cornerstone of his remarkable journey. This approach can be understood through four key pillars: intellectual stimulation, individualized consideration, inspirational motivation, and idealized influence.

Intellectual Stimulation

His dedication to encouraging innovative thinking and continuous learning is palpable. Even when balancing a demanding job, he pursued further education, demonstrating a commitment to staying ahead in technological advancements. This drive sets a powerful example for his team. He creates an atmosphere where questioning the status quo and exploring new ideas are encouraged. This kind of environment inspires creativity and pushes everyone to think beyond conventional boundaries.

Inspirational Motivation

He has an incredible ability to inspire and motivate his colleagues. By sharing his experiences and emphasizing the importance of continuous improvement, he lights a fire within his team to pursue their goals with the same passion and determination. His own story of perseverance and hard work serves as a guiding light, demonstrating that significant achievements are within reach if one remains steadfast and committed.

Individualized Consideration

His approach to leadership is deeply personal. He understands that to drive excellence, a leader must connect with each team member on an individual level. He creates a supportive and collaborative work environment where everyone feels valued. This attention to individual needs strengthens team bonds and boosts morale. His ability to recognize and nurture the unique strengths of each team member upholds his empathetic and inclusive leadership style. This personalized support helps individuals reach their full potential, contributing to the overall success of the team.

Idealized Influence

He leads by example, embodying the values of hard work, humility, and integrity. His leadership is about setting a standard that others can aspire to. By demonstrating these values daily, he earns the trust and respect of his team. His balanced approach—seeing the big picture while meticulously managing operational details—has been crucial in conquering the dynamic renewable energy sector in India. By inspiring an environment where innovation thrives, motivation is high, and individual contributions are valued, he has created a model for successful leadership.

From Vision to Action: Emulating the Leadership Excellence of Kennady Varghese

Drawing on the powerful lessons from his transformative leadership, here are some practical insights for aspiring leaders who want to emulate his success. Each of these strategies offers a roadmap to becoming a more effective and inspirational leader.

Embrace Lifelong Learning

The pursuit of knowledge should never cease. In a world that never stops evolving, staying updated with the latest trends and technologies is crucial. As a leader, your commitment to learning sets the tone for your team. By regularly engaging in professional development, whether through courses, seminars, or self-study, you enhance your own skills and inspire your team to follow suit. This culture of continuous improvement can drive your team to adapt and thrive in changing conditions.

Inspire Innovation

Innovation is about creating an environment where those ideas can emerge and flourish. Encourage your team to think differently and challenge the status quo. Simple strategies like dedicating time to brainstorming, supporting pilot projects, or celebrating creative solutions can invigorate your team. This leads to fresh ideas and makes your team members feel valued and understood, boosting their engagement and loyalty.

Motivate and Inspire

Your energy and passion are contagious. Share your vision and the values that drive you clearly and frequently with your team. When team members understand the 'why' behind their work and see how their efforts contribute to larger goals, their investment in outcomes increases. Recognizing individual and team achievements also adds to this dynamic, creating an environment where motivation thrives on both personal and collective successes.

Personalize Leadership

Each team member is unique, with distinct strengths, aspirations, and learning styles. Spend time understanding these nuances and adapt your leadership approach accordingly. This might mean adjusting your communication style, providing different types of support, or setting customized goals for team members. A personalized approach enhances productivity and deepens your relationships with your team, inspiring a sense of trust and respect.

Lead by Example

Integrity in leadership cannot be overstated. By consistently demonstrating the behaviors and values you expect from your team, you build a foundation of trust. Whether it's showing up on time, meeting deadlines, or handling conflict with grace, your actions set a powerful example. This alignment of words and actions reinforces organizational values and guides your team on expected behaviors and attitudes.

When you integrate these strategies into your way of leading, you'll shape a workplace that truly values and supports everyone who contributes.

Exercise: Blueprint for Leadership Growth

As we explore the journey of leadership, I'd like to share a practical exercise that has been instrumental in my development, inspired by the strategies and principles discussed above. This exercise is designed to help you reflect, plan, and execute your leadership aspirations in a structured and effective manner.

Step 1: Identify Your Vision and Goals

- Reflect on your ultimate professional aspirations. What does long-term success look like for you?

- Write down your vision clearly and set three specific, SMART goals (Specific, Measurable, Achievable, Relevant, Time-bound) that align with this vision. This step creates a clear roadmap towards your desired outcomes.

____

____

____

____

____

____

____

____

____

____

____

Step 2: Evaluate Your Current Position

- Assess your current skills, knowledge, and experience honestly. Identify your strengths and areas for improvement.

- Analyze how your current role can serve as a stepping stone toward your long-term goals and identify any gaps to address.

____

____

____

____

____

____

____

____

____

____

____

____

Step 3: Create a Learning Plan

- Determine key areas requiring enhancement or new knowledge, such as leadership skills, technical expertise, or industry-specific insights.
- Develop a comprehensive plan for acquiring these skills, which may include courses, workshops, reading, or new projects at work.

____

____

____

____

____

____

____

____

____

____

____

Step 4: Develop an Action Plan

- Break your SMART goals into smaller, actionable tasks. Clearly outline specific steps needed to achieve each goal.
- Ensure these steps are practical and well-defined to facilitate progress.

____

____

____

____

____

____

____

____

____

____

____

Step 5: Implement and Monitor Progress

- Start working on your action plan by taking consistent, small steps every day.
- Keep track of your progress and adjust as necessary to ensure continual forward movement.

Step 6: Identify Potential Mentors

- Consider who in your network could serve as a mentor. Look for individuals who embody the qualities you aspire to develop.

- Identify potential mentors from among colleagues, industry leaders, or other admired professionals.

____

____

____

____

____

____

____

____

____

____

Step 7: Engage with Your Mentors

- Set up regular meetings with your mentors to discuss your progress, address challenges, and exchange insights.

- Leverage the guidance and support from experienced mentors, which can be invaluable in your leadership development.

Step 8: Reflect on Your Journey

- Periodically take time to reflect on what you've learned and how you've grown.
- Assess how your skills and perspectives have evolved and consider any new insights gained.

____

____

____

____

____

____

____

____

____

____

____

Step 9: Adapt and Evolve

- Remain flexible and open to revising your strategies as you encounter new opportunities and challenges.
- Adjust your plans as necessary, embracing the non-linear nature of leadership development.

____

____

____

____

____

____

____

____

____

____

____

Wrapping up the reflective leadership mapping exercise, you may have tapped into deeper insights about your own leadership style and values. This journey of self-discovery is far from over; it marks the beginning of a continuous evolution in leadership—learning, adapting, and growing with each experience.

An essential insight to carry forward is making peace your guiding principle in every task. This shift in perspective can transform your approach to life, helping you avoid unnecessary conflicts and inspiring a more harmonious existence both personally and professionally. Leadership is an ever-evolving process, and embracing peace as a core goal can profoundly influence how you lead and live.

Chapter 4

MENTORSHIP AS A CATALYST

"Leadership and learning are indispensable to each other." These words by John F. Kennedy have stayed with me throughout my journey, shaping how I see growth, effort, and leadership. One leader, in particular, has always exemplified this: Mr. Mohan Gandhi- a name that instantly brings to mind the image of a mentor, a learner, and someone who has always believed in the power of effort and guidance.

One of the defining aspects of Mohan Gandhi's leadership is the role mentorship played in his development. He often reflects on his early days, acknowledging that the first decade of his career was typical in many ways—slow and steady, like most. Then came a turning point. Meeting Mr. Sanjaeev Goyal, a General Manager at the time, was a moment of shift, of rethinking what leadership could mean. Goyal's advice was simple yet profound: "Put in the effort. Don't chase the results—they'll come." This struck a chord with Mr. Gandhii, who was used to the constant grind of focusing on immediate outputs. Goyal taught him that success is a patient journey, where effort is the real currency. This wisdom laid the foundation for his approach to leadership—one that is centered on growth and persistence rather than instant gratification.

Another key figure in his journey was Mr. Srinivas, whose mentorship took a different form. Srinivas wasn't interested in the easy tasks or the obvious solutions. His guidance was direct: take on what others shy away from, the tough jobs, the ones that look impossible. It was this embrace of challenges that became the cornerstone of Mr. Gandhi's career. Rather than avoiding the obstacles, he learned to dive headfirst into them, knowing that it was through struggle that real leadership was built. Srinivas didn't just teach him to overcome challenges; he shaped the very way he saw them - as opportunities to grow, adapt, and lead.

Mohan Gandhi's leadership style today is a direct reflection of these lessons. The mentorship he received was a lifeline that pulled him through the hardest parts of his career. He talks openly about the adversity he faced with older employees, the deeply ingrained company culture, and the constant politics swirling around him. The tension between the old-guard employees and the changing domain often left him in situations where politics, more than skill, dictated outcomes. But through it all, the words of his mentors echoed in his mind- focus on the effort, embrace the challenge.

Building on the strong foundation of formative years under the guidance of mentors like Goyal and Srinivas, he transitioned into a leadership role with a distinctive philosophy that has resonated across his team and the wider industry. His leadership shows the strength of having a vision and taking action. He truly believes in thinking big and trying big, and this mindset resonates with everyone on his team.

In his playbook, trust is the foundation of effective leadership. He believes that when people feel secure in their roles, they are more inclined to take initiative and own their contributions. This approach has turned around numerous projects, transforming uncertainty into productivity. "Creating trust by providing job security and confidence" is a practice under the helm of his leadership. For him, pulling team members up to take responsibility means genuinely dedicating tasks to them that challenge their capacities while ensuring they have the support needed to succeed.

This culture of empowerment leads to a unique synergy between the youthful zeal of new technology enthusiasts and the seasoned precision of experienced professionals. He inspires an environment where knowledge is shared freely, where the 'young blood' of technology and innovation is encouraged to blend their ideas with the wisdom of skilled veterans.

Moreover, his emphasis on shared ownership and responsibility is vital. He aligns individual actions with the company's broader interests, crafting a shared vision that each team member is eager to achieve. Each project under his leadership becomes a shared journey, where every success and setback is collectively owned.

As his leadership journey continued, challenges inevitably arose, and few were as daunting as the pandemic. The pandemic posed a unique set of challenges, particularly in terms of manpower retrieval. As the world grappled with uncertainty, he took decisive action to ensure his team's security and continuity. Recognizing the stress and anxiety that the pandemic was causing, he committed to ensuring salaries for the next 12 months. This move was a profound statement of trust and commitment to his team, affirming that no one would be left behind during those testing times.

Moreover, to tackle the operational hurdles introduced by the pandemic, he instituted a system where the team would engage in an extra hour of work daily. This was about pulling together as a unit to sustain the business and support each other. The overtime was a collective effort to thrive against the odds, an embodiment of his belief in teamwork and shared goals.

In dealing with external factors, his approach was similarly nuanced. Understanding and collaboration were his tools of choice. When faced with external challenges, be they logistical, regulatory, or market-driven, he worked to deeply understand the issues at hand. Sitting down with stakeholders, whether they were team members, partners, or even competitors, he strived to see the world from their perspective and find solutions that benefited not just his own team but all involved. This approach entailed elevating the problem-solving process to ensure sustainable and mutually beneficial outcomes.

Conceptualizing the Essence of Mohan Gandhi's Leadership

Delving into his remarkable journey, one recurring theme stands out: a *participative leadership* style built on a foundation of trust and collaboration. He doesn't simply dictate decisions from the top; instead, he invites his team to actively engage in the decision-making process. This participative, or democratic, approach sets the tone for everything from project planning to daily operations.

Sharing Knowledge and Building Trust

At the core of this approach is the value he places on mutual knowledge sharing. His belief is simple—no one has all the answers, and the best solutions come when everyone contributes.

This participative leadership style thrives on trust. His team knows they're not just there to follow orders—they're involved, their opinions matter, and they're expected to take responsibility. By creating an environment of job security and confidence, he ensures that each person feels empowered to speak up, offer suggestions, and be part of the bigger picture. This approach drives ownership. When people feel they have a voice, they're more likely to put their full weight behind the decisions being made.

Success for All

Another defining feature of his participative leadership is the focus on creating a win-win environment. His belief is simple: when the team works together, everyone benefits. This focus on collaboration ensures that no voice goes unheard, and every perspective is valued. Whether tackling a small project or steering through larger challenges, his approach is to seek solutions that benefit both the team and the organization.

Structured Approach to Time Allocation

While he strives as a leader, there's a side of him that brings a remarkable balance to the table. He has developed a time management philosophy that gives him a clear structure for the day. He breaks his time into distinct portions: 10% is spent on regular work, the day-to-day tasks that keep things running smoothly. Then, 40% is dedicated to near-future planning, keeping an eye on what's just around the corner. For longer-term projects, he allocates 25% of his time, ensuring the company is always moving toward bigger goals. And the final 25%? That's reserved for taking breaks and simply letting ideas flow.

This approach to time management offers a glimpse into his work-life balance. It's clear that he believes in the value of breaks as opportunities to refresh his mind and allow creativity to spark. His time isn't consumed by endless tasks. Instead, he creates space for reflection, planning, and growth. This balance helps him stay focused and stress-free, ensuring that he brings his best self to both his work and personal life.

Innovation Through the 80/20 Principle

Then there's his unique take on the 80/20 principle. For him, 80% of the work should be sensible, structured, and planned. But the other 20%? That's where the magic happens. He calls it "nonsensible" work—creative, unconventional problem-solving that might not follow traditional methods but often leads to breakthroughs. He believes this 20% can solve 80% of the challenges he faces. It's this passion for thinking outside the box that often drives the team forward, creating a culture where innovation and sensible work coexist.

Embracing Continuous Learning

What's more, he never sees himself as someone who has all the answers. He's committed to learning from his subordinates, valuing their insights and ideas. This approach to continuous learning shows a level of humility that many leaders lack. This combination of time management, creative thinking, and continuous learning paints the picture of a leader who is actively shaping a balanced, thoughtful, and forward-thinking leadership style.

Vision for the Future

As he looks toward the future, his ambitions are as bold as his leadership style. By 2025, he envisions the company achieving a 300-crore turnover—six times what it was in 2020. This goal is a statement of how far he believes the company can go with the right team behind it. His strategy entails building a team of "100 Warriors"—dedicated, motivated individuals who are ready to push boundaries and create change.

His approach to building this team reflects his broader vision for the company's culture and strategy. By emphasizing recognition and motivation, he ensures that his team is prepared to meet the challenges ahead and driven to exceed them. Each member of the "100 Warriors" is seen as essential to the company's journey toward that ambitious 300 crore goal, embodying the spirit of determination and collaboration that he champions.

From Vision to Action: Emulating the Leadership Excellence of Mohan Gandhi

For anyone looking to imbibe the core principles of his leadership, key lessons stand out—each rooted in practical, actionable insights that can be applied in any role.

Embrace Participative Leadership

One of the most valuable approaches he advocates is participative leadership. This starts with mutual knowledge sharing. To build a truly dynamic team, leaders can establish structured programs or regular meetings where employees from different backgrounds, generations, and expertise come together. These interactions, whether through mentorship programs, cross-training sessions, or innovation workshops, create a platform for the young and tech-savvy to share their knowledge, while more experienced workers bring their years of industry insights to the table.

Involvement in decision-making is another cornerstone. Leaders can create decision-making frameworks that encourage active participation from the entire team. Regular brainstorming sessions, open feedback loops, and collaborative platforms where ideas can be shared and explored are just some of the ways to make this happen.

This sense of inclusion helps employees feel more connected to the outcomes, driving engagement and accountability across the board.

Build Trust and Empowerment

Building trust and empowering teams is at the heart of effective leadership. One of the ways to do this is by ensuring job security and instilling confidence. Leaders can create an environment where clear communication is prioritized, and expectations are consistently articulated. Feedback shouldn't be an afterthought but a regular part of team dynamics, recognizing individual and group achievements in ways that matter—whether through awards, public acknowledgment, or career development opportunities. This kind of recognition makes employees feel valued and motivated to give their best.

Encouraging responsibility is another vital lesson. Leaders need to delegate meaningful tasks, not just busy work. By allowing team members to take charge of projects and decisions, and by supporting them with the right resources and guidance, leaders can help their teams grow. Giving autonomy empowers employees, inspiring a sense of responsibility that fuels creativity and innovation. It also builds future leaders, creating a cycle where empowerment leads to greater confidence and stronger accountability within the team.

Adaptability in Crisis Management

Another crucial dimension emerges, especially evident during challenging times- adaptability in crisis management. During adversity, such as the recent global pandemic, his response was to adapt swiftly, ensuring stability and morale within the team.

Leaders who wish to adopt similar strategies should focus on being flexible and prepared. Developing contingency plans, exploring alternative work arrangements, and maintaining transparent communication with the team are key strategies that can help tackle even the most challenging situations.

Vision and Ambitious Goals

Aspiring leaders should aim to think big when setting their organization's goals. Bold visions inspire teams to push boundaries and embrace challenges. Start by clearly defining ambitious, yet achievable objectives, then communicate these goals in a way that motivates your team to take calculated risks and experiment with new ideas.

Time Management and Work-Life Balance

Effective leaders understand that managing their time well is key to balancing immediate tasks with long-term goals. Allocating time strategically and setting aside portions of the day for routine tasks, short-term planning, long-term goals, and breaks can help ensure you're not caught up in the daily grind at the expense of future progress. Aspiring leaders should experiment with time-blocking methods that prioritize both work responsibilities and downtime. Structuring your time this way helps prevent burnout and allows space for creativity and reflection, which are just as critical as achieving daily goals.

Exercise: Practical Steps to Inspire Growth

As we reflect on the journey of leadership, it's clear that the role of a leader extends far beyond mere management or direction. True leadership is an art that connects today's challenges with tomorrow's aspirations, creating a path that others are inspired to follow.

Step 1: Evaluate Your Engagement Approach

- Consider how you currently engage with your team. Reflect on whether you create an environment that values every voice and encourages knowledge sharing.

- Identify the last significant insight you gained from a team member. Plan how you can foster a more active exchange of ideas to enrich collective outcomes.

____

____

____

____

____

____

____

____

____

____

Step 2: Set Bold, Impactful Goals

- Review your current goals and ask yourself if they are bold enough to push the boundaries of what seems possible and redefine standards within your organization.

- Adjust your goals to ensure they are not only SMART but also bold and visionary, aiming to significantly elevate your team's performance and motivation.

Step 3: Implement Participative Decision-Making

- Examine your decision-making process. Are you involving your team adequately in decisions that affect them and the broader organizational goals?

- Develop and implement a framework that increases team participation in decision-making processes, such as regular brainstorming sessions or decision-making committees that include a diverse range of team members.

____

____

____

____

____

____

____

____

____

Step 4: Nurture an Environment of Trust and Responsibility

- Assess the level of trust and empowerment within your team. Do team members feel secure and empowered to take initiative and ownership of their work?

- Create initiatives that enhance job security and confidence among team members, such as transparent communication about company health and individual performance, or programs that recognize and reward contributions.

____

____

____

____

____

____

____

____

____

____

Step 5: Reflect and Adjust Leadership Practices

- Regularly reflect on your leadership practices and their outcomes. Are they effective? What can be improved?

- Schedule regular feedback sessions with your team and mentors to gain insights into your leadership effectiveness. Use this feedback to adjust your practices, focusing on continuous improvement and adaptation to new challenges.

____

____

____

____

____

____

____

____

____

____

____

As you reflect on these insights, remember that the most effective leaders are those who remain learners at heart, open to growth, and grounded in the belief that every challenge is an opportunity to lead with a participative spirit and resilience.

Chapter 5

PAVING THE WAY

Warren G. Bennis once said, "Leadership is the capacity to translate vision into reality." As I prepare to share the story of a leader who inspired me, these words strike a chord. His story showcases the journey to the pinnacle of professional achievement, highlighting the resilience and strategic savvy that paved his way.

This leader learned the ropes of leadership on a road filled with challenges, each one teaching him invaluable lessons about the corporate world. His approach was methodical, always eager to learn, and profoundly reliant on the collective strength of his team. It was this trust in his colleagues and his never-give-up attitude that saw him through numerous failures and hardships, shaping him into the leader he is today.

He mastered the art of patience, often taking the long road to understand the intricacies of each decision, ensuring that his actions were as informed as they were decisive. This sharp attention to detail and dedication to growth transformed his career and revolutionized the way he viewed leadership.

The man behind this inspiring journey is Subba Rao, Managing Director of Polmor Steel Private Limited.

Subba Rao's professional journey, with its 36 years of rich experience, offers a panoramic view of diverse industry landscapes. From marketing and sales to manufacturing operations, his career has spanned various sectors globally, both in B2B and B2C contexts. His deep understanding of these fields has been a driving force behind significant growth, depicting his adeptness at tackling highly competitive markets.

What truly sets Subba Rao apart is his analytical prowess coupled with extensive expertise in critical business areas. His approach to leadership in marketing, sales, and operations underlines a strong commitment to driving sales, enhancing brand salience, increasing market share, and ensuring profitable growth.

During the pandemic, the true mettle of Subba Rao's leadership came to the forefront. As the world grappled with uncertainty, he was a constant presence at the factory, visiting four days a week. His deep emotional connection to both the company and its people shone brightly during these visits. Rather than leading from a distance, he stood shoulder-to-shoulder with his team, offering both guidance and genuine support.

After the lockdown eased, recognizing the hesitation among his employees to return to work, Subba Rao personally reassured them. He encouraged those living nearby to come back, ensuring they felt safe and valued. His approach was about rebuilding trust and confidence. The company took proactive steps under his leadership, conducting health checks for all employees, which significantly boosted morale and assured everyone that their well-being was a priority.

Looking ahead, Subba Rao has laid out a clear vision for the company's growth, targeting ₹100 crore in sales over the next three years. His strategy focuses on nurturing a motivated team that can carry the organization into the future. This vision includes retaining employees and inspiring a sense of loyalty and commitment, which he believes are key to sustained growth.

Moreover, as industries evolve, Subba Rao is already one step ahead. He has established a program management team dedicated to tracking and adapting to future industry trends. This team's insights are crucial, helping the company proactively shape its strategies to stay competitive and relevant.

Subba Rao emphasizes that truly understanding the heartbeat of a company means connecting directly with those on the front lines. He believes that addressing issues on the factory floor solves problems more effectively and inspires a culture of openness and trust. This approach has been instrumental in steering the organization towards its mission and vision, ensuring everyone is aligned and moving forward together.

He also underscores the importance of avoiding office politics. By keeping the team focused on common goals rather than personal agendas, he has maintained a healthy, productive work environment. Subba Rao's commitment to minimizing politics reflects his dedication to company sustainability and employee cohesion.

Conceptualizing the Essence of Subba Rao's Leadership

Subba Rao's leadership style is *strategic*, infused with elements of *transformational leadership*. His approach is profoundly people-centric, consistently prioritizing the welfare and development of his team members. This trait ensures that his employees feel valued and supported, creating an environment where they can thrive and grow.

Emotional Commitment to Team and Organization

His emotional investment in the company and its people, especially evident during challenging times like the pandemic, highlights his deep commitment to creating a nurturing space for his team. This emotional attachment goes beyond conventional leadership and builds a sense of family and loyalty within the company.

Visionary Goal-Setting

Subba Rao's strategic leadership is evident in his visionary approach to setting ambitious targets, like aiming for 100 Crore in sales. He enhances this goal with practical steps, such as establishing a program management team that stays ahead of industry trends. This forward-thinking strategy ensures that the organization positions itself for long-term success. His analytical prowess allows him to discern key business drivers, crafting strategies that propel growth and solidify the company's competitive stance in the market.

Embracing Innovation and Change

In tandem with his strategic insights, Subba Rao also exemplifies transformational leadership. He has cultivated a culture where innovation thrives and employees are encouraged to embrace changing industry dynamics. His leadership style inspires his team to transcend their limits and actively seek new ways to excel in their roles. By steering clear of office politics and focusing on empowerment, Subba Rao builds a foundation of trust. He empowers his team to make decisions, creating a sense of ownership and commitment to the company's goals.

Together, these elements of strategic and transformational leadership make Subba Rao a leader who inspires his team to march confidently towards the future. His dual focus on setting visionary goals and nurturing a proactive, supportive work environment encourages everyone to contribute to the organization's success and aligns individual aspirations with corporate objectives.

From Vision to Action: Emulating the Leadership Excellence of Subba Rao

Integrating the leadership traits of Subba Rao into your own style can profoundly impact your effectiveness as a leader. By embracing a few key practices, you can cultivate a leadership approach that exceeds expectations.

Focus on Team Development

Firstly, prioritizing team development is crucial. Embodying a strategic leadership mindset means more than just overseeing; it's about enhancing the growth and well-being of your team members. This involves deeply listening to their concerns, offering support, and forging paths for their professional development. By investing in your team's growth, you lay a foundation for organizational success.

Goal Setting and Execution

Setting clear and ambitious goals is another pillar of effective leadership. Strategic leadership requires the vision to set these goals and the precision to craft actionable plans that utilize your team's strengths to achieve them. This clarity in planning helps everyone in the organization understand their role in the larger mission, ensuring all efforts are harmoniously aligned toward shared objectives.

Champion Innovation at Every Level

Creating an innovative culture is essential for staying relevant in rapidly changing industries. Encourage your team to think outside the box and welcome new ideas with enthusiasm. This sparks creativity and positions your organization to adapt swiftly to market changes and emerging opportunities.

Empower Through Trust and Transparency

Lastly, building trust and empowerment within your team can transform the workplace dynamic. A culture where employees feel empowered to make decisions and take initiative leads to a more engaged and motivated workforce. Avoiding office politics and focusing on unity fortifies trust, ensuring that every team member feels valued and recognized for their contributions.

By adopting these practices, aspiring leaders can shape an environment that thrives on mutual respect, collective growth, and shared success, mirroring the impactful leadership style of Subba Rao.

Exercise: Strategic Leadership Alignment

Following the insights into Subba Rao's leadership principles, it's essential to put these concepts into practice. Here's an exercise I've developed, called the Strategic Leadership Alignment Exercise, to help you align your leadership style with resilience, empowerment, and strategic foresight.

Step 1: Strategic Vision Mapping

- Craft a clear and concise vision statement for your leadership role that embodies resilience, empowerment, and strategic growth. This vision should serve as a guide for your actions and decisions.

- Select a crucial organizational goal that connects with your leadership vision. Consider how achieving this goal will ensure both personal growth and team development.

____

____

____

____

____

____

____

____

____

____

____

Step 2: Empowerment Blueprint

- Evaluate your current leadership methods to pinpoint areas where empowerment may be lacking. Ask yourself if there are decisions or responsibilities you could delegate to enhance team autonomy and involvement.

- Develop a specific initiative to increase empowerment within your team. This could be through establishing a mentorship program or a task force that encourages cross-functional collaboration and leadership development.

Step 3: Resilience and Adaptation Challenge

- Visualize a challenging situation, such as a market shift or a new competitor emerging. Craft a response plan that focuses on resilience and adaptability, ensuring your organization can swiftly adjust to new circumstances.

- Review your planned response to the scenario. Assess how well it incorporates resilience and foresight. Fine-tune your strategy to address any weaknesses or gaps, ensuring your approach is comprehensive.

Step 4: Continuous Improvement Commitment

- Establish a continuous feedback mechanism with your team. Utilize tools like surveys, individual meetings, or group feedback sessions to gather insights on the effectiveness of your leadership style and strategies.

- Make a commitment to regularly review and refine your leadership practices based on the feedback received. Keep a record of changes and assess how they contribute to your leadership development and team dynamics.

____

____

____

____

____

____

____

____

____

____

Adopting this structured approach will boost your leadership skills, making you more effective and ready to tackle any challenges that come your way, now and in the future, with confidence and clear thinking.

Chapter 6

BUILDING DREAMS

Every once in a while, you encounter someone whose story shakes you to the core, someone whose very presence proves the immense power of dedication and passion. Every time I think about a leader who has truly touched the community, I feel inspired. I'm talking about Mrs. Kalpana Sankar, the co-founder of Hand in Hand and the Managing Director of Belstar Investment and Finance Pvt. Her story is a real-life example of leading with genuine purpose and heart.

Ralph Nader once said, *"I start with the premise that the function of leadership is to produce more leaders, not more followers."* This leader embodies that idea perfectly. She is a powerhouse of energy, committed to empowering women and children. Every time I delve into Kalpana Sankar's story, I get goosebumps—not just from the scale of her achievements, but from the personal tales of resilience and hope that she's helped to write. Every story showcases how a single person's vision can spark transformation in countless lives.

Kalpana's days are filled with moments that most of us might find ordinary, but through her eyes, they become extraordinary. Imagine visiting a small village where women, once without educational opportunities or economic independence, now run their own businesses and educate their children because she believed in them when no one else did. It's in these moments, seeing the tangible results of her tireless efforts, that the real depth of her impact hits home.

The term 'social entrepreneur' might sound grand, but for those like Mrs. Kalpana Sankar, it's a daily reality marked by courage and an unyielding commitment to societal change. Her battle against child labour and her efforts to uplift underprivileged children are nothing short of heroic. She offers not just the essentials—free food, shelter, and education—but hope for a brighter future.

A few friends and I, having heard about her transformative work, decided to visit her projects and see firsthand the impact of her organization. What we witnessed was astounding. The change she and her team have brought to the lives of children and women in these communities was both heartwarming and profound.

The roots of her journey trace back to 2002 in Kanchipuram, often called the Silk City of India. Here, behind the hum of looms, were the nimble fingers of children, laboring tirelessly. In an industry where children are often seen as cheap labor, many families, lacking a stable income, sent their kids to work as bonded laborers. Witnessing this harsh reality, Kalpana took a decisive step; she started evening schools for these children, sowing the seeds of what would grow into a formidable crusade against child labor.

Initially focused on rescuing children from labor, her vision quickly expanded to embrace whole families, tackling the roots of community health issues, enhancing skills, and, ultimately, nurturing job creation. Today, her initiative, Hand in Hand, is a force of change throughout India.

Under Mrs. Sankar's dynamic leadership, Hand in Hand has made monumental strides, impacting 18 states in India and expanding its reach to seven countries. The organization's achievements are nothing short of remarkable—creating 1.5 million jobs so far, with a mission to reach 10 million by 2025. Their holistic approach spans education, healthcare, skill development, entrepreneurship, financial inclusion, and environmental sustainability, ensuring that each initiative inspires sustainable growth.

In addition to her pioneering work with Hand in Hand, Mrs. Sankar also leads Belstar Investment and Finance Pvt Ltd, a microfinance institution she took under her wing in 2008. Belstar goes beyond being a mere finance company. It acts as a catalyst for change by providing digital financial inclusion and offering collateral-free loans, mainly to women's self-help groups and emerging businesses. Under her guidance, Belstar has evolved into a profitable entity that empowers underserved communities to climb out of poverty and pursue economic independence.

The combined impact of Mrs. Sankar's endeavors in Hand in Hand and Belstar illustrates her unwavering commitment to societal betterment. Leaders like her remind us that with the right vision and dedication, it's possible to forge paths that others might deem impossible.

When I had the opportunity to speak with Mrs. Kalpana Sankar, she shared insights that truly encapsulate the essence of her transformative leadership. She told me, "Everyone in the team should be given an opportunity, even when they make a mistake and want to correct themselves. I will always support my team, take responsibility for any mistakes, and promote individuals to move forward and grow."

Conceptualizing The Essence of Kalpana Sankar's Leadership

As both the Co-founder of Hand in Hand and Managing Director of Belstar Investment and Finance Pvt Ltd, Kalpana Sankar's leadership style is *transformative*, especially in empowering women and children. Her leadership is about nurturing and developing potential, thereby developing their own capabilities to lead. It involves a few critical traits:

Empowerment and Opportunity

True to her word, Kalpana embodies the principle of empowerment. Whether someone makes a mistake or excels, she sees it as an opportunity for them to learn and grow. This philosophy has created a culture of resilience and continuous improvement within her teams. By taking responsibility for setbacks and encouraging her team to push forward, she nurtures an environment where mistakes are seen as stepping stones rather than stumbling blocks.

For instance, through Hand in Hand India, she has provided skill training to over 176,177 women and has empowered them to become self-reliant and economically independent. This entails igniting a belief in their own potential.

Community and Social Impact

Kalpana Sankar's leadership extends far beyond the boardroom; it resonates through villages and across communities. As a social entrepreneur, her focus is on meaningful societal change. Through Hand in Hand, her tireless efforts have eradicated child labor, educated children, and sparked economic opportunities in some of the most underprivileged areas. The scale of her impact is staggering—with

Hand in Hand India having enrolled over 371,196 children in schools and created 9.30 million jobs, each number representing a life moving towards self-sufficiency and empowerment.

Every Challenge is a New Opportunity

Kalpana possesses a remarkable talent for transforming obstacles into opportunities. With a mindset that welcomes challenges, she confronts issues directly, armed with a knack for crafting creative solutions. Her journey from nuclear physics to social entrepreneurship speaks volumes of her capacity to meld scientific rigor with a heart for social change, tackling intricate problems with innovative approaches that make a tangible difference in people's lives.

Asking for Support

Understanding that no one achieves anything alone, Kalpana values the power of community and mentorship. She actively seeks advice and support, building powerful networks that strengthen her initiatives. Her collaborations with global thinkers and leaders, like Percy Barnevik, underscore the importance she places on having strong, supportive alliances to navigate the vast challenges she faces.

Bouncing Back

Perhaps one of her most inspiring traits is her resilience. Kalpana has encountered numerous setbacks but views each as temporary. Her philosophy is one of persistence and perseverance, believing steadfastly in bouncing back with even greater resolve. This resilience has enabled her to scale Hand in Hand's model to a global audience, demonstrating that with determination, any barrier can be transformed into an opportunity for growth.

From Vision to Action: Emulating the Leadership Excellence of Kalpana Sankar

For anyone stepping into the world of leadership, Kalpana Sankar's journey offers a treasure trove of insights. Here's how you can draw from her experiences to enhance your own leadership style:

Embrace Transformative Leadership

Kalpana's ability to inspire her team has been a cornerstone of her success. She leads by example, showing rather than telling, which motivates her team to strive for excellence. As an aspiring leader, focus on being a source of inspiration. Let your actions speak to your dedication and commitment, encouraging your team to reach higher.

True leadership involves lifting others as you climb. Kalpana has always provided her team with opportunities to grow and learn, even from mistakes. For those looking to lead, it's crucial to support your team through challenges and encourage them to embrace new experiences. This builds their confidence.

Focus on Social Impact

One of Kalpana's most impactful strategies has been her focus on social entrepreneurship. Aspiring leaders should aim to make a tangible difference, initiating projects that address critical social issues. Look at Hand in Hand India's approach, which integrates education, healthcare, and job creation, as a blueprint for creating meaningful change.

Kalpana's deep connection with the communities she serves is a powerful model for effective leadership. She is on the ground, understanding the people's needs and aspirations. For upcoming leaders, it's vital to build these connections. Engage directly with the communities you aim to help, listen to their stories, and craft solutions together. This makes initiatives more impactful and sustainable.

Develop Resilience

Resilience shapes leaders, allowing them to grow stronger through adversity. Kalpana Sankar's career shift from a nuclear scientist to a social entrepreneur exemplifies this by turning potential setbacks into expansive opportunities. For any leader, this approach means overcoming challenges and using them as catalysts for innovation and improvement.

Kalpana's transition was not a detour but a deliberate stride into broader societal impact. This perspective is crucial for leaders: when faced with obstacles, identify ways these challenges can elevate your path and expand your influence.

Leadership is a collective journey. Kalpana's ability to connect with global organizations and philanthropists played a crucial role in amplifying her work. Building a supportive network is an essential strategy for success. Surround yourself with mentors and peers who provide insight, challenge your thinking, and support your vision.

Practice Perseverance

The narrative of any leader includes both achievements and obstacles. Kalpana's commitment through various challenges underscores what it means to be steadfast in pursuit of one's goals.

The consistency of Kalpana's efforts underlies her success. She demonstrates that leadership involves continuous dedication to your goals, regardless of the hurdles. It's about maintaining your focus and driving your mission forward every day.

Exercise: Transformative Leadership Toolkit

As we wrap up our exploration of Kalpana Sankar's leadership journey, I'd like to leave you with an exercise that will help you translate the insights gained into actionable steps in your own leadership practice. This exercise is designed to help you internalize and apply the transformative leadership principles.

Step 1: Summarize Key Principles

- Embrace challenges as avenues for growth and innovation.

- Inspire and uplift others, unlocking their potential through your support and guidance.

- Actively seek help and perspectives from mentors and your support network.

- Cultivate resilience and the ability to recover from setbacks.

Step 2: Reflect on Personal Application

- How do you approach challenges?

- In what ways do you support and inspire your team?

- How comfortable are you with seeking help?

- How do you handle setbacks and failures?

____

____

____

____

____

____

____

____

____

____

Step 3: Create an Action Plan

- *Principle: Every Challenge is a New Opportunity*

  Current Approach: How you currently handle challenges.

  Improvement Goal: A specific area for viewing challenges more positively.

  Action Steps: Concrete actions to turn challenges into opportunities.

- *Principle: Transformative Leadership*

  Current Approach: How you currently inspire and support your team.

  Improvement Goal: Ways to enhance your transformative impact.

  Action Steps: Steps to further inspire and uplift your team.

- *Principle: Asking for Support*

  Current Approach: Your comfort level in seeking help.

  Improvement Goal: Areas where you could use more support.

  Action Steps: Steps to strengthen your support network.

- *Principle: Bouncing Back*

  Current Approach: How you handle setbacks.

  Improvement Goal: How to enhance your resilience.

  Action Steps: Steps to improve your ability to recover from failures.

____

____

____

____

____

Step 4: Share Reflections and Action Plan

- Share your reflections and action plan with a trusted colleague, mentor, or leadership group to discuss your goals and receive feedback.

Step 5: Implement and Review

- Over the next month, implement your action plan. At the end of the month, assess your progress:

  What actions were successful?

  What challenges did you face?

  How has applying these principles affected your leadership and team dynamics?

- Write a summary of your experiences and, if possible, continue to share and discuss your progress with your support network to foster ongoing growth and learning.

____

____

____

____

____

____

____

____

____

Reflecting on Kalpana Sankar's journey reminds us that leadership is about making meaningful changes in the lives of others. Her story prompts us to consider what kind of impact we want to make. Are we content to fill roles, or do we aspire to shape futures?

Chapter 7

FORGING AHEAD

In the world of leadership, few people truly stand out, but there's one person whose story encapsulates the essence of inspiring others to greatness. Former US President John Quincy Adams once said, "If your actions inspire others to dream more, learn more, do more, and become more, you are a leader." These words aptly capture the spirit of Mr. Magesh Sekaran, a leader whose journey is as dynamic as it is inspirational.

Magesh Sekaran, the Founder and Business Head of Flashkart India Pvt Ltd, is a rare individual who thrives on new challenges and seeks to make a difference in every situation. From the outset, Magesh's willingness to embrace the unknown set him apart. His passion for his work shines through in every project he undertakes. Rather than avoiding obstacles, he actively seeks them out, knowing that each challenge is an opportunity for growth and innovation.

I first crossed paths with Mr. Magesh Sekaran during a customer-supplier meeting. Right away, his insightful perspectives on the industry and his palpable enthusiasm for his work struck a chord with me. At the time, he held a high-ranking position at one of the leading

OEM companies, a role many would cling to. But Magesh, driven by an entrepreneurial spirit, was ready for a different challenge.

He ventured out on his own to start a supply chain organization dedicated to providing complete solutions for industrial needs. Managing a supply chain business is inherently complex, each day bringing its own set of challenges and lessons. Yet, with over two decades of experience in the industry, Magesh has not only navigated these waters but has also crafted a company that stands out for its resilience and dynamism.

Magesh's strategy in building his business was comprehensive and meticulous. He expertly developed each segment of the supply chain, ensuring his company was equipped to handle the full range of services required in this demanding sector. His holistic approach has established his business as a rare entity in the field, capable of addressing all aspects of supply chain management.

In a particularly reflective conversation with Mr. Magesh Sekaran, I asked him how he managed such significant growth in a short time. His response took us back to the very roots of his journey, revealing how personal hardships shaped the resilient leader he is today.

Magesh's story began in adversity. Growing up in a family that was economically disadvantaged, his life took a drastic turn when his father passed away suddenly from a heart attack. The loss devastated his family both emotionally and financially, leaving a void that urgently needed to be filled. As the eldest son, the responsibility to lead the family out of this turmoil fell on his young shoulders.

"It was a moment of quick, harsh realization," Magesh recounted. "I knew I had to walk the hardest path of my life and take on the family responsibilities my father would have carried. It was about more than just survival; it was about fulfilling the dreams he had for my siblings and me."

This crucible moment in his life taught Magesh some of the toughest lessons about resilience and self-confidence. He stood firm, gathering immense inner strength to support his family and excel in his career. He pushed his limits, setting benchmarks in every role he undertook, driven by a commitment to honor his father's legacy.

"Looking back, I see that journey as my battle to prove 'Survival of the Fittest,'" he said. "Life taught me how to face challenges with a stable mindset, plan meticulously, and execute decisively without succumbing to panic."

Magesh emphasized that embracing full responsibility and accountability for one's actions paves the way to a successful path. His story is a tale of overcoming adversity, upholding the power of determined leadership in shaping a future that once seemed unreachable.

Continuing our conversation, Magesh shared his thoughts on leadership, which further illuminated his approach and philosophy. His leadership style is deeply personal and nurturing, equivalent to that of a parental figure. "I take a parental type of leadership to align with all the team members and work towards a common goal," he explained.

He lives by a simple yet powerful slogan: "I will take care of people, people will take care of my customers, customers will take care of growth, and my growth will take care of employees." This cycle, he believes, is crucial for sustainable and successful leadership. For Magesh, leading with ethics and integrity is non-negotiable. He firmly believes that these values drive the best results in any business environment.

Magesh also spoke about the choices we face in difficult situations. "In every tough situation, we have two paths in front of us," he said. "One, you can get stuck, sulking and asking 'why me?' Or two, you can stand up, create a path for yourself, grow, and show the way for others. The choice is yours."

These words reflect his journey and the mindset that has helped him overcome numerous challenges. Magesh's approach to leadership is about more than guiding his team; it's about fostering a culture where everyone feels supported and valued, paving the way for collective growth and success. His emphasis on ethical leadership and personal responsibility offers a compelling model for aspiring leaders.

Conceptualizing the Essence of Magesh Sekaran's Leadership

Diving into Magesh's insights offers anyone looking to make a real difference a crystal-clear guide. Peering into this guide, we catch a glimpse of the core of *parental leadership* and its powerful influence on your leadership path. This unique perspective can deeply transform your approach to leadership, laying out a blueprint for nurturing a supportive and impactful team atmosphere.

Building Trust and Integrity

At the heart of parental leadership lies the foundation of trust and integrity. Just as parents strive to be transparent with their children to cultivate trust, leaders should embrace honesty in their interactions with team members. This means communicating openly, owning up to mistakes, and sharing both triumphs and setbacks. Such transparency ensures that team members feel valued and included, reinforcing their trust in leadership.

Providing Emotional Support

The role of a parental leader also extends to offering emotional support—understanding and addressing the personal and professional challenges that team members face. This facet of leadership requires empathetic listening and a readiness to provide support when needed, whether it's career advice or encouragement during tough times.

Acting as mentors, parental leaders guide their team members along their career paths, much like a parent supports a child's growth and learning. This mentorship involves more than just leading by example; it's about actively engaging in the professional development of team members, offering guidance, sharing knowledge, and celebrating their progress. This helps in building strong relationships and inspires a supportive network within the team, enhancing overall productivity and satisfaction.

Encouraging Growth and Development

A crucial element of parental leadership is creating the growth and development of team members. Much like parents who guide their children step by step, leaders should emphasize continuous learning and skill development. This involves providing various opportunities for training, attending workshops, and encouraging further education. When team members see that their growth is a priority, it motivates them to strive for excellence and advance in their careers.

Promoting a growth mindset within the team is also vital. This means creating an environment where mistakes are viewed as opportunities to learn rather than failures to be criticized. By encouraging this mindset, leaders help their team members continuously improve, adapt, and innovate. This approach boosts individual confidence and drives the collective success of the team.

Creating a Supportive Work Environment

Another cornerstone of parental leadership is fostering a supportive work environment. Leaders who understand the importance of work-life balance create policies that prioritize the well-being of their employees. This could include flexible working hours, mental health resources, and opportunities for remote work. Such measures show employees that their personal lives and well-being matter, leading to higher job satisfaction and productivity.

In addition to supporting work-life balance, creating a fun and motivating workplace is essential. Just as parents ensure their children have time for play and relaxation, leaders should incorporate elements of enjoyment into the work environment. This can be achieved through team-building activities, celebrating achievements, and nurturing a positive and inclusive culture. When the workplace is enjoyable, employees are more engaged and motivated, leading to a more dynamic and effective team.

Vision to Action: Emulating the Leadership Excellence of Magesh Sekaran

Magesh Sekaran's leadership offers a masterclass in balancing empathy, strategic foresight, and ethical standards. By adopting these practices, aspiring leaders can build teams that are efficient and deeply connected to their shared goals. The following insights provide actionable strategies to help you translate his parental approach into your own leadership journey.

Recognizing Individuality and Ensuring Fair Practices

An essential aspect of parental leadership is recognizing the individuality of each team member. Just as no two people have the same strengths or needs, leaders must tailor their approaches to suit the unique personalities and professional aspirations of their team members. This personalized attention fosters trust and ensures everyone feels valued.

Equally important is the practice of fairness and avoiding favoritism. Leaders who maintain equality and reward merit cultivate trust and boost morale. A fair and transparent environment strengthens team cohesion, allowing members to collaborate effectively and achieve collective success.

Demonstrating Courage and Leading by Example

Leadership often calls for bold decisions, especially when navigating complex or challenging situations. Taking necessary but difficult actions that align with long-term organizational goals requires courage. Much like a parent making tough choices for their family's well-being, leaders must stand firm in their values and principles.

Leading by example is equally powerful. When leaders demonstrate resilience in adversity, take initiative, and act with integrity, they inspire their teams to do the same. This modeling of courage builds respect and confidence, establishing the leader as a role model who motivates others to excel.

Crafting a Vision and Ensuring Stability

A compelling vision is the cornerstone of effective leadership. Much like thoughtful parents plan for their children's futures, leaders must craft strategies and set achievable goals that guide their organizations through challenges. This forward-thinking approach not only addresses current needs but also paves the way for sustained success.

Stability in the workplace is another critical factor. When employees feel secure in their roles and trust in the organization's long-term direction, they become more engaged and committed. A stable environment fosters loyalty and enables individuals to focus on meaningful contributions and personal growth.

Ensuring Accountability

Great leaders take ownership of their actions, setting a powerful example for their teams. This commitment to accountability encourages thoughtful decision-making and builds trust. When team members see their leader taking responsibility, they are more likely to follow suit, fostering a culture of accountability.

Encouraging team members to own their tasks further enhances this culture. When people feel directly connected to the outcomes of their work, they are more engaged and driven. Personal responsibility inspires creativity, innovation, and a deeper commitment to organizational success.

Maintaining High Ethical Standards

Ethical leadership is the bedrock of trust and respect. By consistently demonstrating integrity and ensuring fairness, leaders can cultivate an environment where decisions are viewed as just and equitable. This commitment to high ethical standards reassures team members that they are part of a principled and morally sound organization.

By integrating these principles into your leadership style, you can emulate the essence of Magesh Sekaran's approach, fostering a culture of trust, growth, and accountability while driving meaningful and lasting success.

Exercise: Applying the Principles of Parental Leadership

By embracing these principles, you can shape a workplace that thrives and is poised for future success. As you internalize these key aspects, here's a practical exercise to help you apply the insights learned from Magesh Sekaran's inspiring leadership.

Step 1: Self-Assessment and Reflection

- Reflect on your current leadership style by answering the following questions: How transparent am I with my team?

- Identify areas for improvement and set personal goals to enhance your leadership approach.

Step 2: Building Trust and Integrity

- Implement regular one-on-one meetings with team members to discuss their concerns and share company updates transparently.

- Schedule weekly team meetings to discuss performance, challenges, and future plans openly.

____

____

____

____

____

____

____

____

____

____

____

Step 3: Providing Emotional Support

- Schedule regular check-ins with team members to understand their personal and professional challenges.

- Conduct bi-weekly one-on-one meetings to discuss well-being and career aspirations.

Step 4: Encouraging Growth and Development

- Work with each team member to create a personalized development plan, including specific goals and training opportunities.
- Develop career growth plans and provide access to relevant training programs.

Step 5: Creating a Supportive Work Environment

- Implement policies that promote work-life balance, such as flexible working hours and mental health resources.

- Introduce flexible working hours and provide access to mental health resources.

Step 6: Implementing Fair and Just Practices

- Conduct an audit of current practices to ensure fairness and equity in performance evaluations, promotions, and workload distribution.

- Review promotion criteria to ensure they are based on merit and performance.

Step 7: Demonstrating Courage and Decisiveness

- Create scenarios that require tough decision-making and practice making these decisions while adhering to your values and principles.

- Simulate a crisis situation and discuss the decision-making process with your team.

____

____

____

____

____

____

____

____

____

____

____

____

Step 8: Vision for the Future and Creating Stability

- Organize a workshop to develop a long-term vision and strategy for your team or organization, involving team members in the process.

- Conduct a strategic planning workshop and develop a roadmap with specific goals and milestones.

____

____

____

____

____

____

____

____

____

____

____

As you move forward on your leadership journey, think about the kind of impact you want to create. Are you ready to inspire, nurture, and guide your team with the same passion and integrity that marked Magesh Sekaran's path?

Consider the ways you can create a culture of trust and growth within your organization. How can you support your team in their personal and professional development? What steps will you take to ensure a balanced and fulfilling work environment?

Leadership is a continuous journey of learning and adaptation. It's about making decisions that align with your values, taking responsibility for your actions, and creating a vision that inspires those around you. When you reflect on these questions, remember that the essence of true leadership lies in your ability to connect with your team, empower them, and drive them toward a shared goal.

Chapter 8

FROM LOOMS TO LEADERSHIP

I've often been struck by Michael Jordan's words: *"Obstacles don't have to stop you. If you run into a wall, don't turn around and give up. Figure out how to climb it, go through it, or work around it."* When I think about these words, they remind me of a leader I deeply admire, someone whose life has been all about overcoming walls, no matter how high or daunting.

Her story begins in Kanchipuram, a place known for its rich tradition of silk weaving, where generations of families have passed down the craft. Born into a weaver's family, she grew up surrounded by the hum of looms and the colorful designs that defined her town. As the second daughter, she wasn't exactly welcomed with open arms. At that time, many believed having daughters was more of a burden than a blessing. But her father was different. He held firm to the belief that education was the path forward, and despite the norms of the time, he sent his daughters to college.

In Kanchipuram, where most girls were married off by the age of 15 or 16, this was almost unheard of. Her family was the first to take such a bold step. However, her journey to education wasn't smooth. Just when she was in her final year of college, a family scandal nearly put an end to it all. The relatives and neighbors quickly blamed the situation on their education, saying it was because they were sent to college that such a thing happened. The pressure mounted, and there was serious talk of pulling her out of college as well to avoid any further "disgrace."

For many, this would have been the end of the road. But even then, she had the strength to push back. She had a vision for herself, something greater than the limitations placed on her by tradition, and she wasn't about to let that go. Despite the family pressures and the judgment from relatives, her teachers and college professors stood by her side. They understood her potential and spoke with her family, eventually convincing them to let her continue her studies. With their support, she was able to complete her education and earn her M.Tech degree in Electrical Engineering. But those years were not easy. The constant tension surrounding her education made the journey incredibly stressful. Yet, she persisted, holding on to her dreams despite everything weighing her down.

After finishing her education, she got married. But even after achieving so much academically, new challenges awaited her. She was not allowed to work, and this restriction added more stress to her life. It was a period of waiting, a time when her ambitions had to be put on hold. This stress also affected her personal life. There was a delay in having a child, which led to 4.5 years of treatment before she was finally blessed with a beautiful daughter.

But life didn't give her a moment to relax. As soon as she became a mother, her next challenge emerged: taking care of her newborn while also looking after her mother-in-law, who had fallen ill. It was a demanding time, juggling the responsibilities of motherhood and caregiving, all while tackling the expectations placed on her by her family. Yet through all of this, she kept pushing forward, holding on to the determination that had brought her this far.

As time passed and she continued to manage her family responsibilities, the desire to create something of her own began to grow stronger. Coming from a weaver's family, the art of silk weaving was in her blood. So, she decided to start a business in silk sarees, drawing from her heritage and skills. With perseverance, the business began to do well. She built connections in the export market, opening doors to new opportunities and expanding her reach.

The inspiring leader I am speaking about is none other than Sivasankari, the founder of AR4 Tech. Her journey is one filled with challenges and triumphs, and she embodies the principle that every problem is an opportunity waiting to be understood and solved. Her approach to leadership has always been centered on growth and learning. She once said, "Every issue in my journey is an opportunity, and I have always worked on understanding the technical aspects and developing myself."

Building on the success of her saree business, Sivasankari ventured into something new. With her determination to evolve constantly, she decided to start a herbal hair treatment center in collaboration with a Singapore-based company called Bee Choo Origin. Thus, Herbitaa Hair Treatment Center was born, with one center in Coimbatore, three centers in Bangalore, and another in Chennai. The performance of these centers was extraordinary, generating 8 lakhs of revenue every month from each outlet. Things were going well, and the future looked bright. However, as life often reminds us, challenges are never far away. The COVID-19 pandemic struck, and like many businesses, her centers faced difficulties. Despite her best efforts, the pressures of the pandemic made it impossible to sustain the operations, and ultimately, the business had to close.

Undeterred by these setbacks, Sivasankari was ready to pivot to a new chapter. She joined hands with EMF Innovations as an operational manager, a role that required her to uproot from Chennai and start anew in Coimbatore. This decision was a significant one, involving much discussion and ultimately supported by her husband. At EMF, she faced the formidable task of building the company from scratch—a challenge that proved invaluable when she later founded her own venture, AR4 Tech.

AR4 Tech marked a revolutionary shift in the electric vehicle industry, offering a journey filled with challenges and adventures. This venture honed her ability to manage difficulties and enhanced her skills in negotiating and problem-solving in high-pressure situations. As the pandemic continued to unfold, her resilience was tested once more. COVID-19 struck her personally, and nearly 18 of her employees also fell victim to the virus. With the entire team in isolation and the factory shut down by government order, the pressures mounted. Despite the dire circumstances, Sivasankari was compelled to reach out to her customers. She explained the situation candidly, negotiating for additional time to meet their needs.

Once she recovered, she immediately took action. She visited the collector's office, requesting special permission to reopen the plant. With this permission in hand, she reached out to the few employees who had remained healthy, and together they worked to deliver the products. It might sound simple in hindsight, but the struggle to overcome these hurdles was immense.

Beyond the pandemic, external situations beyond her control created even more significant challenges. One of the biggest was getting approval for a groundbreaking project—converting internal combustion vehicles to electric vehicles (EVs). This was a first for Tamil Nadu, and the lack of established rules and regulations made the journey even more daunting. It took nearly four years of navigating bureaucratic hurdles, advocating for new regulations, and working alongside officials to create the framework for this type of activity.

It was a long and exhausting process, but in the end, her persistence paid off, setting the stage for future innovations in the EV industry in Tamil Nadu. Despite the obstacles, she stayed focused on her vision and worked tirelessly to make it a reality. Driven by this resilience and determination, she adopted a leadership approach that emphasizes personal responsibility and autonomy within her team. She ensures that every individual is given full responsibility for their work, pushing them to take complete ownership of their tasks. Even if they fail, she believes that failure is part of the learning process, encouraging them to grow as future leaders. Her team is made up of students from rural villages, individuals who possess a genuine drive to learn and better their lives. Together with these passionate engineers, they have developed their entire line of kits.

One of the most remarkable aspects of her work is the training program she has implemented for rural women. These women are taught how to convert an internal combustion engine vehicle into an electric vehicle (EV) in just 1.5 hours. The kits are designed to be user-friendly, allowing these women to easily work on converting two-wheelers into EVs. It's a powerful way of creating sustainable livelihoods and empowering women to take charge of their economic futures.

Beyond her professional life, she credits much of her ability to balance work and personal life to her incredibly supportive family.

Time management, she says, would be impossible without them. Her family is her backbone, always encouraging her to shine and reminding her that she has the potential to make a difference in society. Her in-laws, particularly her father-in-law and mother-in-law, have been a constant source of motivation and encouragement. Even her daughter, independent and self-sufficient, allows her the freedom to focus on her work and business. It's this strong support system that has enabled her to thrive in both her personal and professional endeavors, allowing her to lead with confidence and purpose.

Her passion for time management directly feeds into another core aspect of her life: the constant drive to keep learning. She has always been someone who seeks out new knowledge, whether in her professional life or personal interests. Whenever she gets the opportunity, she takes it to learn and grow, always looking ahead. One of her deep-rooted passions lies in exploring herbal and Siddha products. Coming from a country rich in culture and heritage, she has a deep respect for the wisdom of ancient Siddhars and the medicinal benefits of herbs they studied. If time permits, she hopes to work on developing products rooted in this traditional knowledge, with a vision to improve the health and well-being of future generations.

When it comes to defining success, she has a different outlook. She doesn't measure success by the typical milestones of wealth or fame. In fact, she's uncomfortable with the idea of measuring success at all. For her, success is something more personal and ongoing. She doesn't aim to stay in one place or relish in a moment of achievement; instead, she constantly seeks to push further and grow.

What brings her real satisfaction isn't recognition or accolades. It's the impact she sees on the lives of the people who work with her. Knowing that someone in her organization is able to provide good meals for their family and ensure a better education for their children because of the job they have—is what fulfills her. That sense of satisfaction, knowing she has made a tangible difference in someone's life, is the true measure of success in her eyes.

Conceptualizing the Essence of Sivasankari's Leadership

When we take a closer look at her leadership journey, it's clear that her approach is deeply aligned with *resilient leadership*. This type of leadership is all about enduring adversity, embracing change, and rising from challenges with even greater determination. What makes her leadership so compelling is the way she embodies these principles in every aspect of her journey.

Adaptability and Innovation

One of the most defining traits of her leadership is her adaptability. She has tackled a wide range of personal and professional challenges, starting with breaking societal norms to pursue her education. Despite the pressures from her family, she pushed forward, showing that adaptability begins with the courage to stand against the tide.

Later in her journey, when she transitioned from a silk saree business to establishing a successful herbal hair treatment center, it was another example of her ability to pivot and embrace new opportunities.

Persistence Through Challenges

Her whole journey shows the power of persistence. Time and again, she faced challenges, yet she refused to let them stop her. From nearly losing the chance to complete her education to spending four long years working on gaining approval for converting IC vehicles to electric vehicles in Tamil Nadu, her determination never wavered.

Each obstacle only seemed to make her more focused on her goals. This kind of persistence is what defines resilient leadership.

Empowering Others

She has always placed a strong emphasis on empowering those around her. She entrusts her team with responsibilities, encouraging them to take ownership of their work and learn from any missteps. For her, failures are opportunities for growth, and this is a philosophy she instills in her team members. This focus on empowerment is central to her leadership style.

Emotional Intelligence and Support

Another key aspect of her leadership is emotional intelligence. She understands the importance of having a strong support system and recognizes that leadership is about professional success and maintaining balance. Her family has played a crucial role in helping her stay grounded and energized, allowing her to lead with compassion and patience. This emotional intelligence is essential for resilient leaders who need to sustain their energy and focus, especially when tackling challenging times.

Visionary and Forward-Thinking

Her continuous desire to learn and grow is a clear sign of her forward-thinking mindset. Her vision for the future is deeply rooted in the idea of contributing to society in meaningful ways. For her, resilience is about staying focused on the bigger picture, inspiring others to work toward long-term goals, even in the face of immediate challenges.

By breaking down these key traits—empowering others, emotional intelligence, and visionary thinking—we can see how Sivasankari's leadership has been built on a foundation of resilience, adaptability, and forward momentum.

From Vision to Action: Emulating the Leadership Excellence of Sivasankari

Aspiring leaders can draw important lessons from the journey of resilient leadership. These strategies underscore the importance of resilience, purpose, and adaptability, which are critical for tackling the complex challenges of leadership and achieving long-term success

Cultivate a Deep Sense of Purpose

One of the first steps in resilient leadership is identifying your "why"—the core motivation behind your actions. A strong sense of purpose drives leaders to push forward, even during difficult times. Aspiring leaders should take time to reflect on their purpose, aligning their efforts with this driving force. Having this clarity helps maintain focus and enables leaders to inspire and align their team with the shared vision. This deep sense of purpose is what keeps you and your team moving forward, even when challenges arise.

Develop Emotional Intelligence

Emotional intelligence is essential for resilient leadership. It helps manage stress, stay composed, and build meaningful relationships within your team. Leaders should focus on practicing empathy, active listening, and emotional regulation. These skills create an environment where team members feel supported and valued, which nurtures open communication and trust. Handling tough conversations, managing your own emotions under pressure, and showing empathy towards others can create a positive team dynamic, enabling the entire team to handle challenges more effectively.

Strategic Adaptability

Leaders must remain adaptable in the face of constant change. Strategic adaptability involves viewing challenges as opportunities for growth rather than setbacks. Staying informed about industry trends, remaining flexible in your plans, and being open to new ideas can help you respond quickly to changing circumstances. Aspiring leaders should encourage innovation within their teams and be willing to adjust strategies as needed to stay competitive and forward-thinking.

Encourage Continuous Learning and Growth

A commitment to continuous learning is essential for leaders who want to develop resilience. View every challenge as an opportunity for growth, both for yourself and your team. Encourage a culture where curiosity and learning are valued, where mistakes are seen as part of the process, and where individuals feel supported in their pursuit of personal and professional development. By doing this, you ensure that your team is always ready to adapt, innovate, and improve.

Build a Support Network

No leader can do it all alone. Having a strong support network is crucial for both emotional strength and practical guidance. Surround yourself with mentors, peers, and advisors who offer valuable perspectives and insights. These relationships can provide support during difficult times, offering advice that can help you handle complexity and make better decisions. By cultivating these connections, you build a network that strengthens your leadership.

Empower Teams Through Delegation

Empowering your team is about building trust and encouraging ownership. When you delegate effectively, you give your team members the opportunity to take responsibility, make decisions, and learn from their experiences. This creates a culture of accountability and trust. Support your team as they take on new challenges, but give them the autonomy they need to grow. When people feel empowered, they contribute with greater commitment and passion.

Practice Resilient Decision-Making

In times of uncertainty, resilient leaders excel by making informed decisions quickly and effectively. Approach decision-making with confidence, balancing risk with thoughtful consideration of available information. Be open to feedback and willing to adjust your approach when needed. The ability to take decisive action in challenging moments is key to maintaining momentum and ensuring that your organization can move forward, even when faced with unexpected obstacles.

Exercise: A Resilience Framework

To help you embody the essence of resilience, I'd like to guide you through a personal exercise—designed to help you reflect on past experiences, identify your strengths and set clear goals for your continued growth as a leader. This framework is a practical tool that will allow you to strengthen your resilience, and it all starts with self-reflection.

Step 1: Reflect on Past Challenges (30 minutes)

- Take a moment to think about three significant challenges you've encountered, whether in your personal or professional life. Write them down and focus on the following:

  What was the situation, and how did you initially react to it?

  What strategies did you use to get through it?

  What was the outcome, and what did you learn?

____

____

____

____

____

____

____

____

____

Step 2: Identify Strengths and Areas for Growth (20 minutes)

- Once you've reviewed your challenges, look at the strengths that helped you overcome them:

  What are three personal strengths that stood out?

  Where did you feel less confident, or where do you think there's room for improvement?

____

____

____

____

____

____

____

____

____

____

____

____

Step 3: Set Resilience Goals (20 minutes)

- Now that you've identified strengths and growth areas, it's time to set two clear, actionable goals that will help you build your resilience. For example:

  Commit to practicing mindfulness or journaling for 10 minutes every day.

  Make it a goal to learn a new skill relevant to your field every quarter.

Step 4: Develop Your Action Plan (30 minutes)

- Create an actionable plan for each of your goals:

  What are the steps you need to take to reach your goal?

  What resources will you need (e.g., mentors, online courses, or books)?

  Set realistic timelines and milestones to track your progress.

____

____

____

____

____

____

____

____

____

____

____

Step 5: Implement and Reflect Regularly (Ongoing)

- As you implement your action plan, it's crucial to check in with yourself regularly:

  What successes have you experienced so far?

  What challenges are you still facing?

  How can you adjust your approach to stay on track?

____

____

____

____

____

____

____

____

____

____

By following this framework, you'll take actionable steps to build your resilience, learn from your past, and set the stage for future success.

Resilience is something you actively build, step by step, through reflection, growth, and persistence. As you continue to grow in your leadership journey, consider the words of Sivasankari, "My courage is my strength. My father taught me this, and it always keeps me going in any challenging situation." Let that courage be your guide too, as you face whatever lies ahead.

LEADERSHIP INSIGHTS FROM EVERYDAY MOMENTS

Chapter 9

SIMPLE SOLUTIONS, PROFOUND LESSONS

As we begin the final section of the book, I would like to reiterate the words of John F. Kennedy: "Leadership and learning are indispensable to each other." These words hold a powerful truth. Leadership is not a destination; it's a journey where every interaction, every challenge, and every moment presents an opportunity to grow. At its heart, leadership is about people—understanding them, learning from them, and finding inspiration in the most unexpected places.

Every person you meet has a unique story shaped by experiences and insights you might never have encountered yourself. When leaders open their minds to the idea that everyone has something to teach, their perspective expands. Lessons can come from a colleague, a friend, a stranger, or someone you least expect. These moments of learning, often subtle, can reveal fresh ways to approach problems, think creatively, or connect with others on a deeper level.

This willingness to learn from others also changes how teams function. When leaders take the time to genuinely listen and value everyone's contributions, they create an environment where ideas flourish. People feel respected, and that sense of being heard often unlocks their potential to think more openly and share more freely. It's in these spaces of mutual respect that the best ideas are born—not because someone is trying to impress, but because they feel a part of something meaningful.

Sometimes, the simplest insights—the ones that seem almost too obvious—can be the most transformative. They remind us that solutions aren't always grand or complex. Often, they are right in front of us, waiting for someone to notice.

To truly embrace this idea of learning from everyone, leaders need to develop a sense of emotional intelligence and self-awareness. These qualities are the foundation for meaningful growth and connection. When you're willing to engage with perspectives that differ from your own, something shifts. You start to see the biases and blind spots you might not have noticed before. It's a humbling process but one that's deeply enriching.

This kind of learning is about becoming more adaptable. In a world where everything seems to be changing faster than ever, adaptability is key. By paying attention to the experiences and insights of those around you, you start to anticipate shifts and respond with more confidence. Instead of feeling blindsided by challenges, you feel prepared, even when the path forward isn't entirely clear. This ability to adapt can be the difference between thriving in a dynamic environment or struggling to keep up.

Learning from unexpected sources also reminds us how interconnected every role in an organization is. Leadership doesn't belong to a specific title or position. It's something that happens in quiet moments when someone steps up, offers support, or brings a fresh perspective to a problem. When you take the time to observe and learn from others, you begin to notice these moments of leadership everywhere. You see resilience in the way someone handles setbacks, creativity in how they solve a tough problem, and collaboration in how they bring people together.

This broader view of leadership as a shared effort changes the way we approach our work. It creates a sense of belonging and responsibility, where everyone feels empowered to contribute. People stop waiting for instructions and start finding ways to make a difference, no matter their role. As a leader, recognizing and encouraging this dynamic can be transformative. It creates a culture where every voice matters, and every action has the potential to drive meaningful change.

Recognizing the significance of lessons from unexpected sources, I'd like to share a striking experience that underscored this belief for me. It's a vivid memory from my college days involving a professor who had a profound impact on how I view learning and leadership.

Professor K. Krishnamurthy, affectionately known as KK Sir, was a favorite among students. He had a unique way of teaching the Strength of Materials course, often integrating real-world problems into our classroom discussions. This approach created an invaluable sense of collaboration and critical thinking.

One day, he presented us with a puzzle that came directly from a construction site—a live problem that needed urgent solving. A complicated pipe structure had been erected, but there was an oversight. After its installation, it was discovered that some crucial wires needed to be threaded through the already sealed pipes. The construction team was stumped, having worked tirelessly to erect this structure, and now faced the task of integrating these wires without dismantling their hard work.

As the class grappled with the problem of the welded pipe structure, various ideas started to bounce around. Some students thought building a small robot might be the solution to navigating the wires through the complex maze of pipes. Others suggested using a remote-controlled car to pull the wires through. A few even proposed cutting into the pipe at several points to manually insert the wires—a less-than-ideal solution that could compromise the structure's integrity.

The room buzzed with these discussions, each group animatedly sketching out their ideas, calculating feasibility, and debating the potential outcomes. It was exactly the kind of lively brainstorming session that KK Sir had hoped to inspire, where everyone's input was valued and every suggestion considered.

But amidst this whirlwind of ideas, a quiet observer was taking it all in. A janitor, who had been cleaning nearby, had stopped to watch the heated discussion. Without saying much, he slipped away and returned ten minutes later with a surprisingly simple solution.

He approached a nearby engineer and asked for the starting point of the wires. Then, with a bit of unconventional thinking, he tied the end of the wire to the tail of a rat he had managed to catch. He placed the rat at the entry point of the pipe and gently tapped along the pipe's length. Within minutes, the rat had scurried through the maze of pipes, pulling the wire along with it, and emerged at the other end. The solution was as effective as it was unconventional.

What an amazing idea, right?

The Power of Simple Ideas in Leadership

That day left an impression on all of us. As students, we had been so focused on finding a technical solution that we completely overlooked the simpler, more practical ideas right in front of us. The janitor's ingenious approach challenged the way we thought about problem-solving and made us realize how much we could learn from perspectives outside our usual frame of reference.

The lesson here goes beyond the solution itself. It's about the mindset we bring to challenges. Often, we think of leadership and problem-solving as skills reserved for those with advanced knowledge or specialized training. But this experience reminded me that creativity and wisdom can come from anywhere. Effective leadership requires humility—the ability to recognize that everyone, regardless of their role or background, has something valuable to offer.

This story also speaks to the value of thinking differently. The janitor didn't limit himself to conventional methods. Instead, he assessed the resources available and found a practical way to achieve the goal. That kind of lateral thinking, where you approach a problem from an unexpected angle, is something every leader should strive to encourage. When teams feel comfortable sharing out-of-the-box ideas, they're way more likely to come up with creative, flexible solutions—exactly what you need in a fast-changing world.

When leaders actively engage with contributions from all levels of an organization, they often discover that the most impactful solutions come from those who are closest to the daily challenges—the ones who directly interact with the problems at hand.

Moreover, consistently encouraging simple solutions reinforces the idea that not all problems require complex solutions. As leaders, there's a tendency to over-complicate or over-engineer responses to challenges, possibly overlooking the most direct and effective path to a solution. By focusing on stripping back unnecessary layers and getting to the heart of issues, leaders can ensure a more straightforward approach to problem-solving. This streamlines decision-making and enhances clarity in communication and execution, ensuring that the solutions developed are practical and easily implementable.

Embracing this mindset can transform the way teams operate, making them more agile and better equipped to handle whatever comes their way. It's about instilling a sense of clarity and purpose that permeates through every level of the organization, inspiring everyone to look for clear, concise solutions that directly address the core challenges they face.

From Vision to Action: Embracing a Culture of Shared Wisdom

Several practical strategies can help you truly embed these aspects in your leadership style and throughout your organization. These are designed to actively cultivate a culture where every voice is valued and can contribute to the organization's success.

Mentorship and Reverse Mentorship Programs

Mentorship programs have long been a way for experienced professionals to guide others, sharing their expertise and helping less experienced employees tackle their career paths. Reverse mentorship, on the other hand, allows younger or newer employees to offer their perspectives to senior leaders. This dynamic exchange can be incredibly enriching, breaking down hierarchical barriers and creating a culture where learning is a two-way street. Leaders gain fresh insights into emerging trends and technologies, while employees feel their ideas and experiences are valued.

Internal Knowledge-Sharing Platforms

Organizations thrive when knowledge flows freely across teams and departments. Creating spaces—whether digital or in-person— where employees can share insights, lessons, and best practices helps unlock the collective intelligence of the organization. These platforms encourage collaboration and create opportunities for employees to learn from one another's successes and challenges. Over time, this approach helps eliminate silos, ensures stronger connections, and builds a sense of shared purpose within the organization.

Inclusive Decision-Making Processes

Decision-making becomes more balanced when leaders actively seek diverse perspectives. By inviting input from individuals across different levels and backgrounds, leaders can tap into a variety of experiences that enhance problem-solving and creativity. Inclusive practices, such as forming diverse committees or hosting open forums, ensure that everyone feels their voice matters. This approach leads to better outcomes and collaboration within teams, creating a workplace where everyone feels invested in the organization's direction.

Shadowing and Cross-Functional Exposure

Leaders can implement programs that encourage employees to step into each other's roles for a short period to gain firsthand experience of different functions and responsibilities. This kind of shadowing or cross-functional exposure broadens perspectives and helps team members understand the interconnectedness of their work. For leaders, it offers the chance to identify hidden talent and encourage collaboration by giving individuals an appreciation of how their efforts align with broader organizational goals. This practice nurtures empathy and encourages more holistic, innovative approaches to problem-solving.

Storytelling as a Leadership Tool

Leaders can use storytelling as a powerful way to bridge gaps, share lessons, and inspire action within their teams. Encouraging employees to share stories about their experiences—whether they're successes, failures, or moments of creative problem-solving—can provide rich insights for everyone involved. Storytelling humanizes the learning process, making it relatable and memorable while strengthening the emotional connection between team members. When leaders share their own stories of learning from unexpected sources, it models vulnerability and sets the tone for authentic communication.

By embracing these strategies, leaders can cultivate an environment where learning is a shared experience, solutions are enriched by diverse perspectives, and individuals feel empowered to contribute in meaningful ways.

Questions to Guide Your Journey: Reflective Leadership

As you start integrating these strategies into your leadership practice, reflecting on your experiences and approaches can help deepen your understanding and effectiveness. Here are some questions to consider that can kickstart this reflective process in a meaningful way:

- *Have you encountered moments in your leadership journey where unexpected sources provided valuable lessons? Think about those instances. How did they influence your perspective on leadership?*

- *What steps can you take to cultivate an environment where all team members feel safe and valued sharing their ideas?*

- *How do you embody humility in your role as a leader? Humility is foundational for continuous learning. Evaluate how you currently demonstrate openness to new ideas and acknowledge your own limitations. Think about what actions you could take to strengthen this quality, ensuring you remain receptive to learning from anyone at any level within your organization.*

- *When confronted with a complex challenge, do you default to technical or conventional solutions? Reflect on how you can cultivate a habit of considering simpler, perhaps more creative approaches to problem-solving.*

As you think about these questions, try jotting down your thoughts and the steps you want to take next. This simple practice can help clarify your intentions and make your growth as a leader feel more real and achievable.

Chapter 10

THE INNOVATION OF LESS

The pandemic lockdown was a time like no other, a period when the rhythm of daily life shifted in ways none of us could have anticipated. For many of us, it was a time of profound challenges and unexpected learning. The routines we had long relied upon were disrupted, and we found ourselves having to reevaluate even the simplest of decisions. Every choice, from managing household essentials to tackling work-life balance, carried a weight that demanded creativity and precision we weren't used to.

This experience reminded me of how closely the struggles of families during the lockdown mirrored those faced by businesses. Both were forced to adapt to a new reality marked by scarcity and uncertainty. At home, the absence of easy access to basic necessities like groceries or toothpaste meant finding new ways to stretch resources. This wasn't always easy, but it called for a level of ingenuity that was both humbling and eye-opening. Businesses, too, faced their own set of hurdles. Disrupted supply chains and shifting demands forced leaders to pivot quickly and find solutions that often required thinking well outside the usual parameters.

As I reflect on this parallel, it's clear how much the lockdown taught us about resilience and problem-solving. In both homes and workplaces, we learned to adapt, innovate, and work together to overcome the obstacles in front of us. Scarcity forced us to rethink habits we'd taken for granted and to collaborate more effectively, sometimes with people or resources we hadn't considered before.

At its core, this shared experience revealed something deeply human about leadership and adaptability. Whether managing a household or steering a business, the challenges of the pandemic served as a reminder of how much we are capable of when circumstances demand it. More importantly, they showed us the power of looking beyond traditional approaches and embracing creativity in ways that are sometimes as simple as they are profound.

This story reflects how the lessons we learn in the smallest, most ordinary moments can transform the way we think about leadership and problem-solving on a much larger scale.

I remember one particular morning during the early days of the pandemic that brought this lesson home for me, quite literally. It began with what seemed like a small problem but quickly became a moment of clarity that has stayed with me. As I went to brush my teeth, I realized we were almost out of toothpaste. Normally, this would be an issue resolved without a second thought, but in the midst of lockdown, it wasn't so simple. Going out to buy more wasn't an option, and the realization sparked a wave of anxiety.

When I brought it up with my husband, what started as a casual conversation turned into a tense exchange. He expressed his frustration over not having stocked up better, a sentiment fueled by the stress we were both feeling during those uncertain times. It wasn't really about the toothpaste—it was about the larger tension of navigating a world that suddenly felt unpredictable.

Later that day, still preoccupied with the toothpaste dilemma, I mentioned the issue to our maid. She listened with a calmness that stood in stark contrast to the tension that had filled the morning. Her response surprised me. "Please wait for this week; we can manage with what we have," she said with quiet confidence. I couldn't help but feel skeptical. I showed her the nearly empty tube, convinced it wouldn't last beyond the day, let alone an entire week.

Without missing a beat, she assured me there was a way and suggested we wait until the morning to reassess. The next day, after we had all used what we believed to be the last remnants of toothpaste, she took the tube, examined it thoughtfully, and fetched a pair of scissors. With deliberate care, she cut open the container at the top. What she revealed inside made me pause. There was far more toothpaste clinging to the sides than I could have imagined, and she estimated it would last us an entire week.

It was such a simple solution, yet it never crossed my mind. I was struck by how effectively she had solved what had felt like an urgent problem. In that moment, she had done more than stretch a household supply. She had taught me a lesson in resourcefulness that carried weight far beyond our immediate situation. Her approach demonstrated a form of leadership that doesn't rely on access to abundant resources but instead focuses on the ability to creatively and pragmatically maximize what is already available.

This moment made me realize how often we miss what's right in front of us because we're so used to thinking inside the box.

Lessons from Everyday Ingenuity

The story of the maid and the toothpaste tube offers a fresh perspective on leadership that's often overlooked: the power of practical intuition. Leadership doesn't always have to be about bold strategies or cutting-edge innovations. Sometimes, it's about finding straightforward, common-sense solutions that directly address the challenge at hand. This kind of grounded decision-making can be just as impactful, if not more so, in certain situations.

The maid's approach also highlights the importance of observation. Where others might have dismissed the toothpaste tube as empty, she noticed its untapped potential. This ability to truly see what is in front of us and to pay attention to the details that others might overlook is a skill that leaders can develop. Strong observational skills allow leaders to spot opportunities or challenges early, making it easier to respond effectively before issues escalate.

Her initiative also reminds us of the value of empowerment in leadership. By giving people the space to find and implement their own solutions, leaders encourage a sense of ownership and accountability. When team members feel trusted to tackle problems in their own way, they're often more engaged and motivated. This approach leads to quicker and more effective problem-solving, creating a workplace culture where people feel confident in their abilities.

Finally, the maid's decision to wait until the next morning before suggesting a solution is a powerful example of the importance of patience. In a world where the instinct is often to act immediately, taking a moment to pause and fully assess a situation can lead to much better decisions. For leaders, this is a valuable lesson: slowing down can sometimes save time and resources in the long run. Pausing to reflect allows for more thoughtful, deliberate actions that are less likely to result in missteps.

These are key qualities every great leader should have. By focusing on them, leaders can build stronger, more flexible teams and make better decisions when challenges come their way.

From Vision to Action: Building a Leadership Toolbox

In business, where constraints often feel overwhelming, adopting resourceful and strategic approaches can unlock unexpected potential. Here are some practical ways leaders can incorporate these lessons into their leadership style.

Prioritizing and Streamlining Operations

One of the most effective ways to enhance efficiency in resource-constrained situations is to take a closer look at how your organization operates. Are there processes that could be simplified? Tasks that no longer serve the organization's goals? By focusing on core activities and cutting out inefficiencies, leaders can free up resources for more meaningful initiatives. Streamlining is about ensuring that every effort and resource is aligned with what truly matters. This could mean automating repetitive tasks, refining workflows, or reallocating energy toward projects that directly contribute to long-term goals.

Cultivating a Culture of Learning

When resources are limited, investing in the growth of your team becomes even more critical. Encouraging continuous learning ensures that employees are equipped to handle multiple roles and step into new challenges with confidence. Cross-training and skill-sharing within teams can create a more versatile workforce that adapts quickly to shifting demands. By empowering employees to grow and learn, leaders strengthen their teams and ensure the organization remains resilient in the face of change.

Leveraging Strategic Partnerships

Collaborating with other businesses or forming strategic partnerships can create opportunities to share resources, expertise, and ideas. Whether it's working with suppliers to secure better pricing or teaming up with complementary companies to expand market reach, partnerships can help achieve goals more efficiently. This approach allows organizations to benefit from collective strength, often without significant financial investment.

Embracing Frugal Innovation

In challenging environments, creativity often becomes the driving force behind success. Frugal innovation is about finding cost-effective ways to meet customer needs by maximizing existing assets. This could involve rethinking how products are used, exploring alternative materials, or adapting services for new markets. Leaders can encourage their teams to look at problems through a fresh lens, seeking out innovative ways to create value while minimizing resource demands.

Nurturing Agility and Flexibility

In today's dynamic business world, agility is a vital skill for any organization. Leaders who are open to change and ready to pivot their strategies when needed are better positioned to navigate uncertainty. This means building a culture where adaptability is celebrated and teams are encouraged to experiment, iterate, and adjust their approaches as circumstances evolve. Flexibility allows businesses to respond swiftly to market changes, capitalize on emerging opportunities, and mitigate risks effectively.

By using these strategies, leaders can turn challenges into opportunities to grow and innovate. It's all about shifting the focus from what's missing to what's possible—and helping teams see that potential too.

Questions to Guide Your Journey: Harnessing Hidden Opportunities

As you integrate these resourceful strategies into your leadership toolbox, it's valuable to take a step back and reflect on how these principles can be applied within your own context. These reflection questions can help you think more deeply about utilizing your resources effectively and creating a resilient workplace.

- How can you identify and leverage underutilized resources within your organization to enhance efficiency and drive innovation? Begin by reviewing your current assets—people, processes, and technology—to determine if they're fully optimized towards your organization's goals.

- What steps can you take to ensure a culture of continuous learning and adaptability among your team members, ensuring they are prepared to handle changing demands?

- In what ways can strategic partnerships or collaborations benefit your organization, and how can you actively seek out these opportunities?

- How do you currently approach problem-solving in resource-constrained situations, and what changes can you make to encourage more creative and frugal innovation?

These questions are not meant to be answered all at once. They're prompts to guide you as you progress in your leadership journey, helping you align your actions with the values and strategies that can drive meaningful change. Take your time with them, revisit them often, and let them shape how you grow as a leader.

CONCLUSION

As we come to the end of this journey through leadership, I find myself reflecting on the many stories we've shared. These aren't stories of unreachable triumphs or perfect individuals. Instead, they're about real people, leaders who have faced challenges, learned from mistakes, and made decisions that ripple outward in meaningful ways. Through their experiences, we've seen leadership as a deeply personal and evolving process.

What has stood out most through these pages is how leadership is defined by impact. Leadership happens in the moments when you choose to step forward, when you listen deeply, or when you help someone see their potential. It's less about being in charge and more about being present and purposeful in your actions.

Another key lesson I've learned on this journey, and I hope you have too, is that challenges are an inevitable part of leadership. They come in different shapes and sizes—sometimes they're small, frustrating setbacks, and other times they feel like mountains you can't possibly climb. But every challenge holds potential, even if it's hard to see at the moment. These are the times when you grow the most when you're pushed to think in new ways, and when you discover strengths you didn't know you had. Leaders who approach challenges with patience and determination often find that these moments leave them stronger and more capable, not just as leaders but as people. We've come to see mistakes and obstacles as invitations to learn, rather than as failures to fear. It's not easy, but it's worth it.

We've also explored how deeply trust and empowerment shape the success of a leader. When you genuinely invest in the people around you, when you prioritize their well-being, listen to their ideas, and help them develop their strengths, it transforms the dynamic of a team. People feel seen, valued, and motivated to bring their best selves to work.

Creating that kind of supportive and inclusive environment has been one of the most rewarding parts of my own leadership journey. When you recognize the unique strengths of each person, something amazing happens. People feel empowered to step up, and the collective energy of the group becomes unstoppable.

Of course, there are times when resources are tight or challenges come out of nowhere, and it can feel impossible to move forward. These are the moments when resourcefulness and creativity matter most. We've learned that being able to prioritize, adapt, and look for unconventional solutions can turn even the toughest situations into opportunities.

And through it all, adaptability remains one of the most vital skills a leader can develop. The world doesn't stay the same, and neither should we. Being willing to adjust, to rethink strategies, and to let go of what isn't working is what keeps us moving forward. It's a balancing act, but it's also where the magic happens.

I hope the stories and lessons in this book take you closer to this magic—the kind of leadership that feels purposeful, human, and deeply fulfilling. The experiences shared here are meant to spark ideas, challenge assumptions, and give you practical tools to make your own leadership journey meaningful and impactful.

Moving forward, I encourage you to reflect on what resonated with you the most. Think about the moments where you felt a connection, where a story or lesson mirrored something in your own experience. Those moments are where the insights truly begin to take root.

Let it remind you that leadership is about showing up, learning as you go, and staying true to the people and values that matter most to you. It's a journey filled with growth, meaningful connections, and opportunities to make a real difference. As you step into the next chapter, I hope you feel a sense of excitement and possibility for what's ahead. There's so much potential within you and so many ways you can positively impact those around you.

Take what you've learned, step forward with purpose, and lead in a way that leaves the world better than you found it.